TRUTH & ERROR IN *THE DA VINCI CODE*

TRUTH & ERROR IN *THE DA VINCI CODE*

THE FACTS ABOUT JESUS AND CHRISTIAN ORIGINS

MARK L. STRAUSS

AB
AlethinosBooks
San Diego, CA

Cover design by Scott Wildey
Printing by Ken Hamilton and Graphic Business Solutions, Inc.

ISBN 0-9779869-1-8

Printed in the United States of America

Second printing

Library of Congress Cataloging-in-Publication Data

Strauss, Mark L., 1959-
Truth and error in the da Vinci code: the facts about Jesus and Christian origins/ Mark L. Strauss
p. cm.
Includes Quick Answer Guide and Additional Resources
ISBN 0-9779869-1-8
1. Brown, Dan, 1964- Da Vinci code. 2. Mary Magdalene, Saint – In literature 3. Christian saints in literature. 4. Jesus Christ – In literature. 5. Christianity in literature. I. Title.
PS3552.R685434D3 2006
813'.54 – dc22

To Daniel, Jamie and Luke

Ἁγίασον αὐτοὺς ἐν τῇ ἀληθείᾳ·
ὁ λόγος ὁ σὸς ἀλήθειά ἐστιν.

ΚΑΤΑ ΙΩΑΝΝΗΝ 17.17
(John 17:17)

ACKNOWLEDGEMENTS

Thanks are due to Donald Cole, Eric Johnson, George Cox, and Dr. Glen Scorgie, for their careful reading of the manuscript and many helpful suggestions. It is a blessing to have such erudite students, friends and colleagues. I am also grateful to Sherry Stockton, who first introduced me to *The Da Vinci Code* and encouraged me to take up this task.

Special thanks as well to Scott Wildey, for his exceptional cover design and his encouragement and support.

CONTENTS

ABBREVIATIONS

Books of the Bible

Gen.	Genesis
Exod.	Exodus
Lev.	Leviticus
Num.	Numbers
Deut.	Deuteronomy
Josh.	Joshua
Judg.	Judges
Ruth	Ruth
1 & 2 Sam.	1 & 2 Samuel
1 & 2 Kgs	1 & 2 Kings
1 & 2 Chr.	1 & 2 Chronicles
Ezra	Ezra
Neh.	Nehemiah
Esth.	Esther
Job	Job
Ps.	Psalms
Prov.	Proverbs
Eccl.	Ecclesiastes
Cant.	Song of Songs
Isa.	Isaiah
Jer.	Jeremiah
Lam.	Lamentations
Ezek.	Ezekiel
Dan.	Daniel
Hos.	Hosea
Joel	Joel
Amos	Amos
Obad.	Obadiah
Jonah	Jonah
Mic.	Micah
Nah.	Nahum
Hab.	Habakkuk
Zeph.	Zephaniah
Hag.	Haggai
Zech.	Zechariah
Mal.	Malachi

Other Abbreviations

BDAG	*A Greek-English Lexicon of the New Testament and Other Early Christian Literature* (eds. Baur, Danker, Arndt, Gingrich)
c.	*circa,* about
cf.	confer, compare with
DVC	*The Da Vinci Code*
DSS	Dead Sea Scrolls
ed(s).	editor(s)
e.g.	*exempli gratia,* for example
i.e.	*id est,* that is
f., ff.	following page(s)
LXX	Septuagint
MT	Massoretic Text
NHL	*The Nag Hammadi Library in English* (ed. Robinson)
NT	New Testament
OT	Old Testament
passim	throughout, here & there
p., pp.	page, pages
rpt.	reprint
sic	thus, literally
tr(s).	translator(s)
v., vv.	verse, verses

INTRODUCTION

The Da Vinci craze: a cultural phenomenon

The Da Vinci Code – first the book and now the movie – has made a huge cultural impact both in the United States and around the world. Dan Brown's mystery novel has not only met with massive popular success, but has shaken the faith of many with its astonishing claims about Jesus Christ and the origins of Christianity.

The Da Vinci Code claims that almost everything the church says about Jesus Christ is in fact a lie. Jesus was not the Son of God, as the New Testament claims, but merely a human prophet. He taught an esoteric form of religion called Gnosticism, which extolled the sacred feminine and practiced goddess worship. He married Mary Magdalene, who bore a child to him after his death, and his descendants are still around today – a truth kept hidden by the secret society known as the Priory of Sion. The "Holy Grail" was not the cup Jesus passed to his disciples at the Last Supper, but was Mary herself, who carried the blood offspring of Jesus. Jesus intended Mary, not Peter or the other apostles, to be his successor. The early church, which was misogynist (hating women) and patriarchal (male-dominated), suppressed the earliest writings about Jesus and created its own version of the facts. The result is that the Bible we have today was written by these "winners" and so presents just one side of the story, an inaccurate and distorted view of Jesus. Many other gospels, suppressed by the church, tell the real story about Jesus and Mary Magdalene.

No wonder the book is controversial! If these claims were true, the Christian faith as practiced by millions today would be a sham based on lies and fabrications. But *The Da Vinci*

Code is in fact not true. Its fundamental claims have no historical foundation, and the book is riddled with historical and factual errors – some laughably bad. Yet many Christians do not have the knowledge or resources to respond to these errors. This little book is meant to give you access to those tools. The book is arranged in a simple question and answer format for quick reference to the key issues raised by *The Da Vinci Code* related to Jesus Christ and origins of Christianity. Footnotes alert the reader to scholarly support and original sources. At the end of the book, a Quick-Answer Guide with page reference allows readers to find answers quickly to their questions.

In selecting questions, I have focused primarily on claims related to Jesus Christ, the New Testament documents, and the history of early Christianity. This emphasis is for two reasons: (1) these are the issues that concern most Christians, and (2) my expertise lies in the field of New Testament and the Jesus movement of the first century AD. While these are my primary concerns, I also touch on issues like Leonardo's *The Last Supper,* the Priory of Sion and the Templar Knights, which have direct bearing on the truth or falsity of the book's claims.

As you read, please remember that all truth is ultimately God's truth. This book is *not* intended to be a propaganda piece in support of traditional Christianity, but rather to set the historical record straight by allowing readers to examine the evidence for themselves.

Plot summary of *The Da Vinci Code*

The slipcover of *The Da Vinci Code* summarizes its plot:

> While in Paris on business, Harvard symbologist Robert Langdon receives an urgent late-night phone call. The elderly curator of the Louvre has been

> murdered inside the museum, a baffling cipher found near the body. As Langdon and a gifted French cryptologist, Sophie Neveu, sort through the bizarre riddles, they are stunned to discover a trail of clues hidden in the works of Da Vinci – clues visible for all to see and yet ingeniously disguised by the painter.
>
> The stakes are raised when Langdon uncovers a startling link: The late curator was involved in the Priory of Sion – an actual secret society whose members included Sir Isaac Newton, Botticelli, Victor Hugo, and Da Vinci, among others. Langdon suspects they are on the hunt for a breathtaking historical secret, one that has proven through the centuries to be as enlightening as it is dangerous. In a breathless race through Paris, and beyond, Langdon and Neveu find themselves matching wits with a faceless powerbroker who appears to anticipate their every move. Unless they can decipher the labyrinthine puzzle in time, the Priory's ancient secret – and an explosive ancient truth – will be lost forever.

The "ancient truth" turns out to be Jesus' marriage to Mary Magdalene and Mary's identity as the Holy Grail – a secret supposedly suppressed by the Catholic Church through the centuries. The story becomes personal for its main characters when it is revealed that Jacques Saunière, the murdered curator and Grand Master of the Priory of Sion, is in fact the grandfather of Sophie Neveu, so that Sophie turns out to be one of the long lost descendants of Jesus and Mary.

When Langdon and Neveu become suspects in the murder, they gain the help and protection of Leigh Teabing, a former British Royal Historian and expert on the Holy Grail. Teabing turns out to be a key apologist for the myths about

Mary and Jesus, and many of the revisionist statements concerning Jesus, Mary, and early Christianity come from his lips. Langdon, however, fully concurs with these claims, lending his substantial (if fictional) credentials as a Harvard Ph.D. to the book's premises.

Dan Brown's sources

So where did Dan Brown get his ideas about Jesus, Mary and the Holy Grail? In fact, almost nothing in *The Da Vinci Code* is original. At one point in the book, the character Leigh Teabing states that "The royal bloodline of Jesus Christ has been chronicled in exhaustive detail by scores of historians" (*DVC,* p. 253 [= p. 273 paperback edition][1]). Several of these so-called "historians" are then named, volumes that in fact served as Dan Brown's main sources. These are:

- **Michael Baigent, Richard Leigh and Henry Lincoln, *Holy Blood, Holy Grail*** (New York: Dell, 1983).
  This must be regarded as Dan Brown's primary source, so much so that two of the authors have recently sued Brown for using their ideas.[2] *Holy Blood, Holy Grail* is the source of the claim that Jesus was married to Mary Magdalene, that Mary is the Holy Grail, and that this secret was guarded by the Priory of Sion. In a wink to his source, Brown names one of his main characters Leigh Teabing, borrowing the last name of one author and producing an anagram of another (Baigent).

---

[1] Page numbers for *The Da Vinci Code* identified in this book refer to the hardback edition; page numbers for the paperback edition are enclosed in square brackets.
[2] David Stringer, "'Da Vinci Code' author accused in London court of taking material from previous work," Associated Press, 2/27/06; accessed at signonsandiego.com/news/world/20060227-0853-davincicode-lawsuit.html.

- **Lynn Picknett and Clive Prince, *The Templar Revelation: Secret Guardians of the True Identity of Christ*** (New York: Simon and Schuster, 1998).
These authors, who describe themselves as experts in the paranormal and UFOs, picked up many of their theories from *Holy Blood, Holy Grail* and took them further. The book identifies Jesus as a mystic trained in Egypt who practices Egyptian sex rituals with Mary Magdalene. Picknett recently wrote a second volume called *Mary Magdalene: Christianity's Hidden Goddess* (New York: Carrol and Graf, 2003).

- **Margaret Starbird, *The Woman with the Alabaster Jar: Mary Magdalen and the Holy Grail*** (Rochester, VT: Bear, 1993), and ***Goddess in the Gospels: Reclaiming the Sacred Feminine*** (Rochester, VT: Bear, 1998).
Starbird acknowledges that she was "won over" by the theories of *Holy Blood, Holy Grail* and became a believer in the Grail story. Many of Dan Brown's assertions concerning the sacred feminine and goddess worship come from Starbird's work.

None of these authors are trained historians, and the theories they propose are not taken seriously by reputable scholars.[3] These works would better be categorized as tabloid journalism or speculative pseudo-history. They draw on legends, revisionist histories, and pure hearsay to build dubious theories that claim to be the "hidden truth"

[3] In addition to these pseudo-historical works, there are works of serious scholarship challenging traditional Christian perspectives, claiming, for example (1) that Jesus was merely a human prophet; (2) that orthodox Christianity, like Gnosticism, was just one of many competing "Christianities"; (3) that the New Testament canon has no special claim as authoritative Scripture; and (4) that women originally held a much higher status in the Jesus movement, but that patriarchal leadership suppressed them. We will respond to these claims in subsequent discussion.

suppressed by powerful establishment authorities. The methodologies utilized are highly questionable:

(1) The author will propose a theory based on the flimsiest of evidence, sometimes using a "what if…" or "isn't it possible…?" kind of statement – inviting the reader to consider an alternate historical possibility. This "what if" quickly becomes the historical "fact" upon which other equally dubious theories are built.

(2) Generalized statements like *"Historians claim…"* or *"All scholars agree…"* are used to introduce views held by few, if any, real scholars. When sources are cited, they represent less-than-credible authorities.

(3) Snippets of historical sources are cited without attention to their historical context. For example, in *The Da Vinci Code* Gnostic literature is quoted with little understanding of the nature or context of Gnosticism.

(4) Very late or apocryphal sources are introduced as hard evidence despite their legendary nature. Medieval legends about Mary Magdalene composed a thousand years after Christ hardly constitute reliable historical evidence for her life.

(5) Legitimate ancient sources that contradict the author's theory are simply ignored, thus withholding critical evidence from the unsuspecting reader.[4]

The result is an historical house of cards built on little or no hard evidence. Unfortunately, naïve or unsuspecting readers are often drawn into the charade, unable to recognize illogical arguments or disreputable sources. Since *The Da Vinci Code,* similar books have multiplied as other authors attempt to capitalize on Dan Brown's success – making it even harder for uninformed readers to discern truth from fiction.

---

[4] Some similar points are made by Hank Hanegraaff & Paul Maier in *The Da Vinci Code. Fact or Fiction* (Wheaton IL: Tyndale, 2004), pp. 35-36.

Brown's characters repeatedly point out that "history is always written by the winners," and claim to be presenting "the *other* side of the Christ story" (*DVC,* p. 256 [276]) – the version suppressed by the powerful majority. It is certainly true that all history is written from the perspective of its chroniclers, and so must be carefully scrutinized to discern fact from fiction. Unfortunately, no such critical scrutiny appears in *The Da Vinci Code*, which promotes fanciful theories without any real evidence to back them up.

Isn't *The Da Vinci Code* just a story – a work of fiction?

I have heard a number of people ask why everyone is making such a fuss, since *The Da Vinci Code* is simply a work of fiction. Just enjoy the story, they say – a thrilling murder mystery – and stop your whining!

In fact, *The Da Vinci Code* claims to be much more than a work of fiction. The opening page states in large letters "FACT," and affirms the existence of the secret society known as the Priory of Sion, founded in AD 1099 (a claim we will see is bogus), followed by the statement that "All descriptions of artwork, architecture, documents, and secret rituals in this novel are accurate." The implication is that the symbols and hidden messages discovered in artwork throughout the book and the secrets related to Jesus Christ and the origins of Christianity are in fact true.

While characters in the book like Robert Langdon and Leigh Teabing are fictional, they are depicted as authoritative scholars describing well-established and defensible historical realities. In fact, these "scholars" more often spout tabloid nonsense and wild speculative theories that no credible historian or scholar would affirm.

The genre Dan Brown has chosen for *The Da Vinci Code* is historical fiction, and as Amy Welborn points out, "in writing historical fiction, the author makes an implicit deal with the reader. He or she promises that, while the novel concerns fictional characters engaged in imagined activities, the basic historical framework is correct."[5] Yet in *The Da Vinci Code,* this covenant is repeatedly broken, as supposedly reliable characters make blatantly false or misleading statements. This is not just harmless fiction; it is either gross historical incompetence or intentional deception.

But there is another reason we cannot simply dismiss *The Da Vinci Code* as "just a story." Whether from lack of knowledge or from gullibility, many people are actually believing it. I have heard people say, "I never knew all that about Jesus and Mary Magdalene!" Others report that friends or family members have had their doubts about Christianity confirmed by the claims of the book. So whether or not Dan Brown intends the book to be taken seriously (his public comments suggest that he does[6]), in fact people *are* taking it very seriously.

When someone sits down to read H. G. Wells' *War of the Worlds,* they will immediately identify it as science fiction and not panic about space aliens tromping through their living room. It is harmless and entertaining science fiction. Yet when Orson Welles read the book on live radio on October 30, 1938 and many people poured into the streets in terror – whether through gullibility or ignorance – someone had to say, "Wait! It's not true!" In the same way, although *The Da Vinci Code* is just a story, many people are taking it very seriously. And this demands a response.

---

[5] Amy Welborn, *Decoding Da Vinci. The Facts Behind the Fiction of The Da Vinci Code* (Huntington, IL: Our Sunday Visitor, 2004), p. 21.

[6] For interviews with the author and his own comments see www.danbrown.com.

CHAPTER ONE

THE IDENTITY OF JESUS CHRIST

The most controversial of all claims in *The Da Vinci Code* is that the early church believed that Jesus was merely a human prophet, but that the Roman emperor Constantine and the 4th century church transformed him into a deity for political reasons. Constantine's reason, it is said, was to unify the Roman empire around an entity whose power was unchallengeable.

***The Da Vinci Code* claims:**

"At [the Council of Nicea, AD 325]....many aspects of Christianity were debated and voted upon – the date of Easter, the role of the bishops, the administration of sacraments, and, of course, the *divinity* of Jesus,...until *that* moment in history, Jesus was viewed by His followers as a mortal prophet...a great and powerful man, but a *man* nonetheless. A mere mortal." (*DVC,* p. 233 [253]; spoken by Teabing)

"Jesus' establishment as 'the Son of God' was officially proposed and voted on by the Council of Nicaea... establishing Jesus' divinity was critical to the further unification of the Roman empire and to the new Vatican power base. By officially endorsing Jesus as the Son of God, Constantine turned Jesus into a deity who existed beyond the scope of the human world, an entity whose power was unchallengeable." (*DVC,* p. 233 [253]; spoken by Teabing)

Did the Council of Nicea turn Jesus into a god?

This claim is so outlandish one wonders how Dan Brown's book got through its editorial review at Random House. Perhaps no one who reviewed the book had ever studied early Christianity (or read the New Testament!).

The Council of Nicea (AD 325) did not create the deity of Christ, but only confirmed and clarified what Christians had been proclaiming for centuries. There is indisputable evidence that Christians were worshipping Jesus as divine in the first century, two hundred and fifty years before the Council of Nicea.[1] Consider the exalted statement of Christ's deity at the beginning of the Gospel of John:

> In the beginning was the Word, and the Word was with God, and the Word was God. He was with God in the beginning. Through him all things were made; without him nothing was made that has been made. (John 1:1-3)

This passage – written before the end of the first century – identifies Jesus as the pre-existent "Word" (Greek: *logos*) who was at the same time distinct from the Father ("with God") yet fully divine ("was God"). This description of distinct persons within the one Godhead became the foundation for the doctrine of the Trinity, where Father, Son and Spirit are separate persons yet one God. Such profound statements of deity are not unique to John's Gospel. The New Testament epistle to the Hebrews (*c.* AD 67) states that, "The Son is the radiance of God's glory and the exact representation of his being, sustaining all things by his powerful word" (Heb. 1:3). Similarly, the apostle Paul, writing around AD 62, opposed false teachers at Colosse by

---

[1] See especially Larry W. Hurtado, *Lord Jesus Christ. Devotion to Jesus in Earliest Christianity* (Grand Rapids: Eerdmans, 2003).

affirming the supremacy of Christ: "For in Christ all the fullness of the Deity lives in bodily form" (Col. 2:9).

It is important to note that these are not isolated statements, but affirmations spread across the broad range of early Christian authors and communities. The deity of Christ is taught both explicitly and implicitly throughout the New Testament. John 1:3 identifies the Word (= Jesus) as the pre-existent Creator of the universe. Just as Genesis 1:1 declares that "in the beginning *God* created the heavens and the earth," so here it is the Word through whom the Father created all things. For similar statements of Jesus as the Creator, see Hebrews 1:2, Colossians 1:16 and 1 Corinthians 8:6.

At the same time, the New Testament affirms Jesus' true humanity. The prologue of John's Gospel goes on to say that "the Word became flesh and made his dwelling among us" (John 1:14). "Flesh" here means a true human being. The New Testament book of Hebrews strongly emphasizes Jesus' full humanity: "Since the children have flesh and blood, he too shared in their humanity…he had to be made like his brothers and sisters in every way, in order that he might become a merciful and faithful high priest in service to God" (Heb. 2:14, 17). In the NT Gospels we see a far more human portrait of Jesus than in the later apocryphal and Gnostic gospels. Jesus displays a range of human emotions, including anger, indignation, sorrow, grief and amazement. In the Garden of Gethsemane Jesus said "My soul is overwhelmed with sorrow to the point of death" and begs the Father to "take this cup from me" (Mark 14:34, 36). (We will discuss Jesus' humanity further when we examine the Gnostic gospels in Chapter 3, pp. 44-45.)

Yet along with this true humanity, Jesus' amazing words and deeds – climaxing in the resurrection – convinced his earliest followers that he was far more than a mere man. Evidence that Christians were worshipping Jesus as divine at a very early date comes from a passing reference in First Corinthians 16:22, where the apostle Paul uses the Aramaic expression *maranatha. Mar* is the Aramaic word for "Lord" and the expression means, "Our Lord, Come!"[2] Why is this phrase so significant? Aramaic was the language spoken by Jesus and his earliest Palestinian followers. Paul's use of an Aramaic expression in a letter written in Greek (around AD 55) indicates that he is using a *prayer* drawn from the Aramaic-speaking church before him. We therefore have hard evidence that shortly after the resurrection, Jewish Christians were already praying to Jesus and addressing him as "Lord" – both clear indications of his deity. This shatters the idea that the worship of Jesus as divine came about in a later Greek or pagan context where it was common to worship many gods and goddesses.

Those who followed the apostles also strongly affirmed the deity of Christ. Ignatius (*c.* AD 50-117), writing in the first decades of the second century, said "There is only one Physician...God become man...Jesus Christ Our Lord."[3] Early in the second century, the unknown author of 2 Clement begins his homily: "Brethren, it is fitting that you should think of Jesus Christ as of God — as the Judge of the living and the dead" (2 Clement 1:1). The second century apologists followed the Gospel of John in identifying Jesus as the preexistent *Logos,* the Word made flesh. As we move forward into the third and fourth centuries, statements of Christ's deity become even more explicit.

We also have secular evidence for early Christian belief in the deity of Christ. Around AD 112, Pliny the Younger,

---

[2] That the phrase is meant to be a prayer to Jesus is indicated by its use in a prayer at the end of the Eucharist meal in the *Didache* (10:6), an early church document dated near the end of the first century, and also by the parallel expression in Revelation 22:20, "Come, Lord Jesus." See Hurtado, *Lord Jesus Christ,* pp. 172-176.

[3] Ignatius, *To the Ephesians* 7.2.

governor of Bithynia (modern northern Turkey), wrote a letter to the Roman emperor Trajan for advice on how to deal with Christians who were brought to him for trial. Summarizing Christian practice, he wrote that, "They were in the habit of meeting before dawn on a fixed day, when they would recite in turn a hymn to Christ, as to a god, and would bind themselves by an oath...."[4] Pliny's statement confirms that in the early second century Christians were worshiping Jesus as divine.

In summary, Dan Brown shows complete disregard for the historical record when he claims that the early church viewed Jesus as a mere mortal until the Council of Nicea in AD 325 deified him.

What really happened at Nicea?

The Da Vinci Code gets many other facts about the Council of Nicea badly wrong. The Council was not called by Constantine to consolidate his power, but rather to unify the church and to settle the Arian controversy. Arius, a presbyter in Alexandria, Egypt, began teaching that Jesus was a created being, inferior to God. This caused an uproar in the church, and a council was called to restore unity. The discussion did not center on whether Jesus was a mere mortal – even Arius acknowledged that the Son of God was an exalted being who had existed before time began. The question was whether the Son was co-eternal and equal with the Father. Arius' views were overwhelmingly rejected,[5] and the Council issued a decree confirming that:

[4] Pliny the Younger, *Letters* 10:96.7.

[5] While Arius' views were soundly rejected, significant debate centered around whether Jesus was made of the "same substance" (*homoousios*) as the Father or of "similar substance" (*homoiousios*). The question, then, was not the deity of Christ, but the precise nature of his relationship with the Father.

> "We believe in...one Lord, Jesus Christ, the Son of God, the only-begotten of the Father, that is, of the substance of the Father, God from God, light from light, true God from true God, begotten, not made, of one substance with the Father...."

Nor was this conclusion "a close vote," as Teabing asserts *(DVC*, p. 233 [253]). Of the approximately three hundred bishops, only two of Arius' closest supporters, Secundus and Theonas, refused to sign the Creed.[6]

It is important to note that none of this had anything to do with Mary Magdalene, goddess worship, Gnosticism, or the Gnostic gospels, all of which Dan Brown claims Constantine suppressed at the Council of Nicea. It is not Gnostics, but modern Jehovah's Witnesses, with their denial of the full deity of Christ, who follow the teachings of Arius. The Gnostics would have rejected Arius, and vice versa.

Apart from the fact that Dan Brown's history is badly skewed, the scenario of Constantine deifying Jesus for political reasons makes little sense. A much better way to unify the empire around a single, all-powerful leader would have been for Constantine to declare *himself* divine, something Roman emperors had done before him.

Equally odd and illogical is the fact that while *The Da Vinci Code* rejects Christ's deity, it *affirms* the deity of Mary Magdalene as a goddess. One would have thought Brown's purposes would have been better served by keeping Jesus a god and so the equal to his "goddess" Mary! Teabing's statement, however, is probably not meant to be logical, but to shock the reader.

---

[6] All the major works of early church history deal with the Council of Nicea. For points made here, see Leo Donald Davis, *The First Seven Ecumenical Councils* (Wilmington, DE: Michael Glazier, 1987), pp. 33-80; Mark A. Noll, *Turning Points. Decisive Moments in the History of Christianity* (Grand Rapids: Baker, 2000), pp. 47-64.

CHAPTER 2

CONSTANTINE AND THE BIBLE

The Da Vinci Code claims that the Bible we have today was put together for political reasons in the 4th century AD. The emperor Constantine, it is said, chose those books that supported his political agenda and suppressed other gospels that presented the "real Jesus."

A closer look will reveal that this revisionist history does not hold up under critical scrutiny.

> ***The Da Vinci Code* claims:**
>
> "...The Bible did not arrive by fax from heaven...The Bible is the product of *man*, my dear. Not of God. The Bible did not fall magically from the clouds. Man created it as a historical record of tumultuous times, and it has evolved through countless translations, additions, and revisions. History has never had a definitive version of the book." (*DVC,* p. 231 [250-51]; spoken by Teabing)
>
> "The fundamental irony of Christianity! The Bible, as we know it today, was collated by the pagan Roman emperor Constantine the Great." (*DVC*, p. 231 [251]; spoken by Teabing)
>
> "Constantine commissioned and financed a new Bible, which omitted those gospels that spoke of Christ's human traits and embellished those gospels that made him godlike. The earlier gospels were outlawed, gathered up, and burned." (*DVC*, p. 234 [254])
>
> "...the early Church needed to convince the world that the mortal prophet Jesus was a *divine* being. Therefore, any gospels that described *earthly* aspects of Jesus' life had to be omitted from the Bible." (*DVC,* p. 244 [264]; spoken by Teabing)

Did Constantine support Christianity for political reasons?

Constantine the Great (*c.* AD 274-337) is famous as the first Roman emperor to convert to Christianity, ending state sanctioned persecution of the church. Constantine granted tolerance to Christians in AD 313 and adopted Christianity as the state religion in AD 324. A few scholars have claimed that Constantine's conversion was not genuine, but was purely a political move. It is certainly true that the empire's transition from paganism to Christianity was gradual, and that Constantine remained tolerant toward paganism. Yet Constantine's personal devotion and his many actions in favor of the church – supporting the clergy, restoring church property, building churches, commissioning copies of Scripture – suggest an authentic conversion experience.[1] *The Da Vinci Code* is correct that Constantine was not baptized until his death bed, but certainly wrong that he was "too weak to protest" (*DVC,* p. 232 [251]). Rather, it was common in that day to delay baptism under the assumption that baptism washed away past sins but not future ones.

The Da Vinci Code also claims that Constantine shifted Christian worship from Saturday (the Jewish Sabbath) to Sunday as part of the worship of the sun (*DVC,* pp. 232-233 [252]). This is false. The New Testament shows Christians already worshiping on the first day of the week (Sunday) during the first century, hundreds of years before Constantine (Acts 20:7; 1 Cor. 16:2; Rev. 1:10). Christians worshipped on Sunday because it was the day of the resurrection, not because they worshipped the sun god. *The Da Vinci Code*

---

[1] On the authenticity of Constantine's conversion, see Paul L. Maier, *Eusebius. The Church History* (Grand Rapids: Kregel, 1999), pp. 373-375. For biographies of Constantine, see A. H. M. Jones *Constantine and the Conversion of Europe* (New York: Macmillan. 1949, rpt., 1979); Lloyd B. Holsapple, *Constantine the Great* (New York: Sheed & Ward, 1942); Michael Grant, *Constantine The Great: The Man and His Times* (New York: Macmillan. 1993); Ramsay MacMullen, *Constantine* (New York: Croom Helm 1969).

also claims that many Christian symbols have pagan origins (*DVC*, p. 232 [252]). It is certainly true that Christians sometimes took over pagan symbols and invested them with Christian meaning. But this is true of any culture. No culture wipes clean its history at the moment of conversion. Rather, symbols and holy days are *transformed* with new meaning and significance.

The important question is not whether some symbols have non-Christian roots, but whether the *present meaning* is pagan or Christian. Would anyone claim that Christians are today worshipping pagan gods because the date of Christmas and the origins of the Christmas tree may (perhaps) go back to the Roman feast of Saturnalia? Of course not. Origin or etymology does not determine the present meaning of a word or concept. Otherwise we would have to assume that a "pineapple" is a kind of apple, "butterflies" are made of butter, and everyone who uses the word "Sunday" is a secret worshipper of the sun. This is nonsense.

Did Constantine commission a "new Bible"?

Constantine had nothing to do with which books were included in the Bible, and he did not commission a new Bible. The New Testament Gospels were considered inspired Scripture long before Constantine was born. Constantine did support Christianity by commissioning the production of *copies* of Scripture.[2] But he was not involved in discussions concerning the *canon* of Scripture (see next question).

---

[2] Eusebius, *Life of Constantine* 4:36. Constantine also took action against certain groups viewed as heretical, including the Valentinians, followers of the teaching of Valentinus, the most prominent of the second century Gnostics (see Eusebius, *Life of Constantine* 3:64).

How was the canon of Scripture determined?

In *The Da Vinci Code,* Teabing claims that "History has never had a definitive version of [the Bible]." This statement, though a misrepresentation, raises the important question of the *canon* of Scripture. The word "canon" means a rule or standard and, in the context of Christianity, refers to those books considered by the church to be authoritative Scripture.[3] When were these books collected and recognized by the people of God?

We should note, first of all, that the earliest Christians already had a Bible, the *Hebrew Scriptures,* what Christians today call the Old Testament (OT). There is solid evidence that by the first century the OT books we have today had already achieved canonical status.[4] Jesus often quoted from the OT and referred to it as the "Law of Moses, the Prophets and the Psalms" (Luke 24:44), a description representing the three sections of the Hebrew canon: the Law, the Prophets and the Writings.[5] The Jewish historian Josephus identified this same three-part canon as those books "which are justly believed to be divine."[6]

---

[3] For much greater detail on the formation of the canon see Bruce Metzger, *The Canon of the New Testament: Its Origin, Development and Significance* (Oxford: Clarendon, 1987) and F. F. Bruce, *The Canon of Scripture* (Downers Grove: InterVarsity, 1988). For a shorter treatment with reference to *The Da Vinci Code,* see Michael Green, *The Books the Church Suppressed. Fiction and Truth in* The Da Vinci Code (Oxford & Grand Rapids: Monarch Books, 2005).

[4] See R. Beckwith, *The Old Testament Canon of the New Testament Church* (Grand Rapids: Eerdmans, 1985).

[5] There was also a widespread tradition in Judaism that the prophetic voice of God had ceased after the post-exilic prophets: "With the death of Haggai, Zechariah and Malachi, the latter prophets, the Holy Spirit ceased out of Israel" (*Tosefta Sotah* 13:2; cf. Talmud *b. Sanhedrin* 11a; Josephus, *Against Apion* 1.40-41).

[6] Josephus, *Against Apion* 1.8 §§38-41. Josephus refers to twenty-two books and categorizes them as the Law (five books), the Prophets (thirteen books) and four books which "contain hymns to God, and precepts for the conduct of human life" (the Writings). Though ordered differently than our Old Testament, this threefold division represents the same books. A similar ordering is given by Origen (cited by Eusebius, *Church History,* 6.25).

Jesus was recognized by the early Christians as the Jewish Messiah, the fulfillment of God's promises made to Israel in the Old Testament. These believers searched the Hebrew Scriptures to discover prophecies fulfilled by Jesus. Even the name Jesus *Christ* points back to the Old Testament, since the Greek term *Christos* is a translation of the Hebrew *Mashiach* ("Messiah"), meaning "Anointed One" and referring to the promised king from the line of David.[7] This is an important point to keep in mind, since the New Testament writers all look back to the Hebrew Scriptures as the authoritative Word of God and consider their own writings to describe its fulfillment. By contrast, the Gnostic documents tend to reject or ignore the Old Testament. We might ask which movement likely arose from the original teaching of Jesus of Nazareth (the first century Jew!), one that embraced the Hebrew Scriptures or the one that rejected them?

The established authority of the Hebrew Scriptures gave the early Christians precedent to view their own foundational documents as authoritative Scripture. After all, the account of God's promise for a Savior in the Hebrew Scriptures found its natural complement in the authoritative accounts of its fulfillment in the New Testament. At a very early date, the four Gospels, the epistles of Paul and other apostolic writings were collected, copied and circulated as authoritative texts. Already in 2 Peter 3:15-16 we see Paul's letters being compared to "the rest of Scripture" (i.e., the Old Testament). Similarly, in 1 Timothy 5:18 Jesus' teaching from Luke 10:7 appears to be identified as Scripture.

Impetus to define the canon more precisely came in the form of controversy. Marcion, a second century teacher with proto-Gnostic tendencies, came to believe that the god of the Old Testament was an inferior god who had created the evil material world. He compiled a truncated canon made up only

---

[7] See 2 Sam. 7:11-16; Ps. 89:3-4; Isa. 9:6-7; 11:1-5.

of portions of Luke's Gospel and certain Pauline letters. The church responded with its own canon discussions. Lists of authoritative Scripture began to appear about this time. The Muratorian fragment, a canonical list dating from about AD 160, named the four Gospels, the thirteen letters of Paul, two letters of John, Jude, and the Revelation.[8] About this same time Irenaeus, bishop of Lyons, identified a similar collection, including First Peter.[9] In the early third century, Origen named all twenty-seven books of our New Testament canon, while acknowledging that six were disputed by some, including Hebrews, James, 2 Peter, 2 and 3 John, and Jude.[10] The first list that is identical to our twenty-seven New Testament books appears in an Easter letter written by Athanasius of Alexandria in AD 367.

What is important to note is that while there were discussions concerning the exact limits of the canon continuing into the fourth century AD, the core of the New Testament – and the four Gospels in particular – attained unquestioned authority by the middle of the second century. Only a few books that did not make the canon were even mentioned in canon discussions (Barnabas, Hermes, Wisdom of Solomon), and *none* of these were the Gnostic writings that *The Da Vinci Code* claims were the earliest Christian documents. The claim made by the book – that the New Testament was a large amorphous body of literature (containing over eighty gospels!) until Constantine and his cronies cut out the books they didn't like – is simply false. The four canonical Gospels were firmly established as *the church's gospels* centuries before Constantine and decades before the Gnostic gospels were written. We will say much

[8] The Muratorian canon also names two additional works, the *Wisdom of Solomon* and the *Apocalypse of Peter,* though it raises doubts about the latter.
[9] For details see Bruce, *Canon,* 170-77. Irenaeus never produces a definitive list, but alludes to these works.
[10] Cited by the early church historian Eusebius, *Church History,* 6.25.8-14.

more on the relationship between the New Testament Gospels and the Gnostic gospels, and their respective dates, in Chapter 3, pp. 38-44.

In summary, the church did not *remove* the Gnostic gospels from the New Testament, because they were never seriously considered for inclusion in it. This is because these writings had no direct link to Jesus and his earliest followers and because they taught doctrines contrary to the teachings Jesus had passed on to his disciples.

Has the Bible "evolved through countless translations, additions and revisions"? (*DVC*, p. 231 [251])

This claim, made by Teabing, is a muddled statement unbefitting a real historian, which greatly confuses the process by which the Bible came down to us. The three terms, "translations, additions and revisions," must first be unpacked. Let's start with *translations.* The Old Testament books were originally written in Hebrew (with a few sections in Aramaic), and the New Testament books in Greek. English Bible translations (or "versions") produced today are either revisions of previous English Bibles or translations made directly from the Hebrew and Greek. For example, the *New Revised Standard Version* (NRSV, 1990) is a revision of the *Revised Standard Version* (RSV, 1952), while the *New International Version* (NIV, 1978, '84) – the most widely used English Bible today – is a version translated directly from the Hebrew and Greek.[11] It must be added, however, that even those versions that are revisions were produced by biblical scholars working with the original Hebrew and Greek texts. Indeed, the entire purpose of a revision is to update the

[11] For a summary of the history of the English Bible, see Dick France, "The Bible in English: An Overview," in *The Challenge of Bible Translation. Communicating God's Word to the World* (eds. Glen G. Scorgie, Mark L. Strauss and Steven M. Voth; Grand Rapids: Zondervan, 2003), pp. 177-97. This volume has many other helpful essays on the theory, history and practice of Bible translation.

text to make sure it accurately represents the meaning of the original Hebrew or Greek.

The implication of Teabing's statement that the Bible "evolved through countless translations" is that each version is a translation of a translation of a translation, and so on, so that the result is like the children's game "telephone," where the message gets more and more garbled along the way. This is simply not the case. Bible versions today are produced using the earliest and most reliable Hebrew and Greek manuscripts available.

So what about the claim of "countless additions and revisions"? The implication is that the Bible has been changed again and again throughout history to meet the needs of the church. Here again the statement is a gross misrepresentation. As noted above, Bible translations today utilize the earliest Hebrew and Greek manuscripts available. Over the centuries before the invention of the printing press, scribes meticulously copied the biblical texts by hand in order to preserve and protect God's Word. A hand-copied document is known as a *manuscript*. Inevitably, errors are made in the process of hand-copying a document, and the biblical texts are no exception. The methodology known as *textual criticism* has been developed by scholars to reconstruct as accurately as possible the original text.[12]

[12] For Old Testament textual criticism, see E. R. Brotzman, *Old Testament Textual Criticism: A Practical Introduction* (Grand Rapids: Baker, 1994). For more detail, see E. Würthwein, *The Text of the Old Testament* (2nd ed.; Grand Rapids: Eerdmans, 1995); E. Tov, *Textual Criticism of the Hebrew Bible* (2nd ed.; Minneapolis: Fortress, 2001). For NT textual criticism, see the brief surveys in D. A. Black, *New Testament Textual Criticism. A Concise Guide* (Grand Rapids: Baker) and J. H. Greenlee, *Introduction to New Testament Textual Criticism* (2nd ed.; Peabody: Hendrickson, 1995). For more detail, see K. Aland and B. Aland, *The Text of the New Testament* (2nd ed.; Grand Rapids: Eerdmans, 1989) and B. Metzger, *The Text of the New Testament. Its Transmission, Corruption and Restoration* (3rd ed.; New York & Oxford: Oxford UP, 1992).

For the Old Testament, textual critics compare the Hebrew manuscript tradition known as the Massoretic Text (MT) with the Greek versions of the Septuagint (abbreviated LXX), and now the Dead Sea Scrolls (DSS), which contained many biblical manuscripts. For the New Testament they compare more than five thousand ancient Greek manuscripts containing parts or the whole of the New Testament. Textual critics also examine ancient Greek lectionaries (Scripture passages arranged for church reading), early versions of the New Testament translated into languages like Latin, Syriac, Coptic, Armenian, and Slavonic, and the writings of the early church fathers, who frequently quote Scripture.

Several summary points may be made about the reconstruction of the original text of Scripture:

(1) The vast majority of manuscript differences are minor issues of grammar or spelling that have little impact on the meaning of the text.[13]

(2) No point of Christian doctrine is in doubt because of manuscript variations.

(3) The Bible boasts better manuscript support than any other ancient work of literature. For example, the first six books of the *Annals* of the famous Roman historian Tacitus are preserved in only one manuscript, dating from the sixth century AD. Many of the greatest classical Greek works exist in only a few manuscripts dating from the Middle Ages. Even

---

[13] The only two textual variants of any length in the New Testament are the longer ending of Mark (16:9-16) and the account of the woman caught in adultery (John 7:53-8:11). For discussion of these texts, see B. Metzger, *A Textual Commentary on the Greek New Testament* (2nd ed. Stuttgart: United Bible Societies, 1994), pp. 102-106, 187-189. In terms of different "editions" of biblical books, there are only two issues of significance. The OT book of Jeremiah appears in two different editions, one approximately one-sixth shorter than the other. The shorter version is represented in the Septuagint and in some manuscripts of Jeremiah found in the Dead Sea Scrolls. A somewhat longer edition of the NT book of Acts also exists in the so-called Western manuscript tradition (see Metzger, *Textual Commentary,* pp. 222-236).

the best preserved ancient documents cannot compare to the New Testament. Homer's *Iliad,* sometimes called the "bible" of the ancient Greeks, is preserved in only about 650 manuscripts, most dating from the second and third centuries – one thousand years after the *Iliad* was written.[14] Compare this to the five thousand New Testament manuscripts, some copied within decades of the original writings.

(4) The great majority of scholars agree that we have a highly reliable manuscript tradition, something very close to what the original authors wrote. Figures of 95-97% accuracy beyond reasonable doubt are often cited for the New Testament, and 90% or so for the Old Testament.[15] This is a remarkably reliable textual tradition, considering the age of these sources, and refutes the claim of *The Da Vinci Code* that "History has never had a definitive version of the book" (*DVC,* p. 231 [251]).

(5) There is no "cover-up" related to the text of the Bible. The standard critical editions of the Hebrew Old Testament and the Greek New Testament used by scholars of all religious and philosophical viewpoints list variant readings in their margins. The standard Hebrew text is the *Biblia Hebraica Stuttgartensia* (5th edition). The two standard critical Greek New Testaments are the Nestle-Aland *Novum Testamentum Graece* (27th ed.) and the United Bible Societies' *The Greek New Testament* (4th ed.). Any student with Greek or Hebrew competence can see for themselves the minor variations within the manuscript tradition.

Is the Bible a human or a divine book?

It is certainly true, as *The Da Vinci Code* asserts, that the Bible did not arrive from heaven by fax or fall magically

[14] Metzger, *Text of the New Testament,* p. 34.

[15] These figures are cited by W.W. Klein, C. L. Blomberg and R. L. Hubbard, Jr. in *Introduction to Biblical Interpretation* (Nashville: Nelson, rev. 2003), p. 122.

from the clouds (*DVC,* p. 231 [250]). No biblical scholar or informed Christian claims that it did. The Bible claims rather to be *inspired by God,* human authors communicating God's message to his people (2 Tim. 3:16-17; 2 Pet. 1:20-21). Like Jesus, the living "Word," the written Word of God claims to be both *fully human and fully divine.*

Evidence for the divine origin of the Bible may be seen in (1) its extraordinary unity, (2) its many fulfilled prophecies, and (3) its transforming power. We will briefly discuss each of these.

(1) The unity of the Bible is evident in the fact that, although made up of sixty-six books written by more than forty authors over a 1500-year period, it demonstrates an extraordinary unity of theme from beginning to end. This theme may be summed up as *the actions of God in bringing salvation to the world through Jesus Christ his Son.*

The book of Genesis begins with God's creation of a perfect world, which, because of the disobedience of Adam and Eve, falls into a state of sin and decay. The Old Testament books that follow reveal God's promise and plan to raise up a Savior who will defeat sin and death and bring restoration to all of creation. The New Testament presents the fulfillment of that promise through the coming of Jesus, who lived a perfect life and died on the cross to pay the penalty for humanity's sins. The Bible concludes with a description of the completion of God's plan: the destruction of evil, sin and death, the final salvation of God's people, and the creation of a new heaven and a new earth. Every book, every story, and every character in the Bible fits into this grand drama of redemption. This great unity suggests that the Bible is more than just a library of disparate writings containing human reflection on religious themes. It is rather the design and accomplishment of the God who is bringing his purpose and plan to fulfillment.

(2) The divine character of the Bible is also evident in its many fulfilled prophecies. The Old Testament predicts that the Messiah would be born in Bethlehem (Micah 5:2) to a descendant of David (Isa. 9:7; 11:1). We are told his public ministry would center in Galilee (Isa. 9:1), that he would enter Jerusalem at the climax of his ministry riding on a donkey (Zech. 9:9), that he would be rejected by his own people (Isa. 53:1-3; Zech. 12:10), and that he would suffer and die for their sins (Isa. 52:13-53:12). All of these prophecies and more were remarkably fulfilled by Jesus Christ.

(3) In the end, the transforming power of the Bible may be the greatest evidence for its divine origin. The Spirit of God working through the testimony of Scripture has changed the lives of millions of people throughout history. My challenge to skeptics is to check out the Bible for themselves. I never warn my students *not* to read the so-called "heretical" or apocryphal literature that Dan Brown claims are the earliest Christian writings. Rather, I encourage them to read and compare these works to the Bible. This is because God's Word has no rival, either literarily or spiritually. Read this Book beside the great Greek and Latin classics; read it beside the Apocrypha; read it beside the Gnostic gospels; read it beside the Koran or the Book of Mormon. I am convinced its divine origin and authority will be evident to those willing to hear and be transformed by its life-giving message.

CHAPTER 3

GNOSTICISM AND THE "LOST GOSPELS"

The Da Vinci Code claims that the New Testament Gospels should not be viewed as either the earliest or most reliable of the early Christian writings. More than eighty other "gospels" presumably existed, but Matthew, Mark, Luke and John were chosen because they supported the theology of the powerful and patriarchal church, which subsequently destroyed these other writings. Among these gospels were the Gnostic writings, which supposedly revealed the true human Jesus, an enlightened feminist who encouraged worship of the "sacred feminine" and appointed Mary Magdalene to be his successor.

As we shall see, all of these claims are false.

***The Da Vinci Code* claims:**

"...More than eighty gospels were considered for the New Testament, and yet only a relative few were chosen for inclusion – Matthew, Mark, Luke and John among them..." (*DVC,* p. 231 [251]; Teabing speaking)

"The scrolls highlight glaring historical discrepancies and fabrications, clearly confirming that the modern Bible was compiled and edited by men who possessed a political agenda – to promote the divinity of the man Jesus Christ and use His influence to solidify their own power base." (*DVC,* p. 234 [254-55]; Teabing speaking)

"'These are photocopies of the Nag Hammadi scrolls, which I mentioned earlier,' Teabing said, 'The earliest Christian records'." (*DVC,* p. 245 [266]; Teabing speaking)

Were the New Testament Gospels chosen over more than eighty others?

The claim that there were eighty other "gospels" all vying for inclusion in the New Testament is wildly exaggerated. The New Testament Gospels – Matthew, Mark, Luke and John – are by far the oldest and most reliable records we have of the historical Jesus. All four can be reliably dated before the end of the first century. The so-called "apocryphal gospels" were written decades, and even centuries, later. For details, see the following questions. See also the discussion of the canon of Scripture in Chapter 2, pp. 27-31.

Are the Dead Sea Scrolls "lost gospels"?

One comment made in the *The Da Vinci Code,* though not directly relevant to the historicity of the Gospels, must be noted since it reveals Dan Brown's general lack of historical competence. In discussing the so-called "lost gospels," Teabing says, "Fortunately for historians…some of the gospels that Constantine attempted to eradicate managed to survive. The Dead Sea Scrolls were found in the 1950s hidden in a cave near Qumran in the Judean desert…." (*DVC,* p. 234 [254]). This is a remarkably naïve statement, especially coming from Sir Leigh Teabing, supposedly a British royal historian! The Dead Sea Scrolls were discovered in 1947, not the 1950s, and are Jewish, not Christian writings. They were a library of texts buried by the Jewish community at Qumran, which flourished from the second century BC until they were destroyed by the Romans around AD 70. Most scholars identify the Qumran sectarians as Essenes, a group within Judaism mentioned by the Jewish historian Josephus and other writers. The scrolls have been very helpful for understanding the first century world in which Jesus lived, but they are not gospels, and they tell us nothing about Jesus himself.[1]

What are the "lost books" of the New Testament?

This question has been partly answered under our discussion of the canon of the New Testament in Chapter 2. The literature known as the New Testament Apocrypha is a diverse collection of writings composed by a variety of groups within early Christianity ("Christianity" used here in its broadest sense of any group claiming to follow Jesus Christ). None of these works can be reliably dated to the first century AD, so all are later than the New Testament books. They are also *pseudonymous,* that is, written under an assumed name. The Gospel of Peter, for example, was not written by Peter but by an unknown Christian, probably in the middle of the second century.[2]

Within the New Testament Apocrypha are a number of works identified as "gospels."[3] Most of these are not like the New Testament Gospels in the sense of accounts of the life and ministry of Jesus. Some involve stories and sayings of Jesus; others are dialogues between Jesus and the disciples;

---

[1] English translations of the Dead Sea Scrolls may be found in F. G. Martinez, ed., *The Dead Sea Scrolls Translated: The Qumran Texts in English* (2nd ed. Grand Rapids: Eerdmans, 1996) and G. Vermes, ed., *The Dead Sea Scrolls in English* (rev. edition. Harmondsworth: Penguin, 2004). For the significance of the scrolls in relationship to early Christianity, see J. H. Charlesworth, *Jesus and the Dead Sea Scrolls* (New York: Doubleday, 1995); James VanderKam and Peter Flint, *The Meaning of the Dead Sea Scrolls: Their Significance for Understanding the Bible, Judaism, Jesus, and Christianity* (San Francisco: HarperSanFrancisco, 2002).

[2] For texts of the New Testament Apocrypha and bibliography see J. K. Elliott, ed., *The Apocryphal New Testament* (Oxford: Clarendon, 1993); W. Schneemelcher, ed., *New Testament Apocrypha* (2 vols.; rev. ed.; Louisville: Westminster/John Knox, 1991-92).

[3] For brief discussion of the Apocryphal Gospels, see R. J. Bauckham and S. E. Porter, "Apocryphal Gospels," in *Dictionary of New Testament Background* (eds. C. A. Evans and S. E. Porter; Downer's Grove, IL: InterVarsity, 2000), pp. 69-78. For the texts themselves, see previous note.

still others are theological essays on a variety of subjects. Some of these apocryphal gospels arose within the second century movement known as Gnosticism, and so may be called "Gnostic gospels" (see the next two questions).

What is Gnosticism?

Gnosticism is the modern name given to a variety of religious groups that shared the same basic worldview and certain core beliefs.[4] There is significant debate today whether Gnosticism is pre- or post-Christian in origin.[5] While the basic pantheistic[6] and dualistic perspective shared by these groups was certainly pre-Christian, Gnosticism itself appears to have developed in the early second century AD as an attempt to adapt Christianity to this worldview.

Gnostics were syncretistic, drawing together many components of Christianity and other religions. Their belief system arose from the philosophical foundation of Platonism, a dualistic perspective that contrasted the pure spiritual realm and the material world. The Gnostic foundation myth concerned the supreme god, or *Pleroma* (meaning, "fullness"), who was wholly transcendent and pure spirit. Emanating from this god were many *aeons*, or lesser spirit beings. One of these (sometimes called the *Demiurge*), created the fallen material world. In contrast to Judaism and Christianity, where God's physical creation is "very good"

---

[4] For a summary article on Gnosticism and bibliography, see D. M. Scholer, "Gnosis, Gnosticism," in *Dictionary of the Later New Testament* (eds. R. P. Martin and P. H. Davids; Downer's Grove, IL: InterVarsity, 1997), 400-12. For more depth, see G. Filoramo, *A History of Gnosticism* (Oxford: Blackwell, 1990); A. H. B. Logan, *Gnostic Truth and Christian Heresy: A Study in the History of Gnosticism* (Peabody, MA: Hendrickson, 1996); P. Perkins, *Gnosticism and the New Testament* (Minneapolis: Fortress, 1993).

[5] See Edwin Yamauchi, *Pre-Christian Gnosticism: A Survey of the Proposed Evidences* (2nd ed.; Grand Rapids: Baker, 1983).

[6] Pantheism is the belief that God and the material world are one and the same thing, and that God is present in everything.

and human beings – unified as body, soul and spirit – bear the image of God, Gnosticism saw the material world as evil and the physical body as something to escape.

Gnostics taught that a person gained salvation through secret knowledge (*gnōsis*) of their true spiritual identity and heavenly origin. Salvation is not a gift from God on the basis of Christ's death on the cross, as Christianity teaches, but is the discovery within oneself of this true spiritual identity. The goal of Gnosticism is to return to the realm of pure spirit.

Jesus Christ became in Gnosticism one aeon or emanation, sent to teach humans about their true spiritual nature. Gnostics rejected the *incarnation* of Christ (that God became a true human being) and the saving significance of his death on the cross. Salvation does not come through sacrifice and atonement, but through *gnōsis*. Unlike in Christianity, where all people bear the image of God and in Christ there is "neither Jew nor Greek, slave nor free, male nor female" (Gal. 3:28), Gnostics viewed themselves as superior spiritual beings by virtue of their secret *gnōsis*.

Gnosticism became a major rival to Christianity in the second and third centuries. The most influential Gnostics were the Valentinians, whose beliefs arose from the teachings of Valentinus (*c.* 100-153), a prominent second century leader in the church at Rome. A number of early church writers labeled the movement heretical and wrote against it, including Justin Martyr (*c.* 100-168), Irenaeus (*c.* 130-202), Clement of Alexandria (*c.* 150-216), Tertullian (*c.* 155-230) and Origen (*c.* 182-251). Until the 20th century, most of our knowledge about Gnosticism came from these opponents. The Nag Hammadi Codices, discovered in 1945 in Egypt, contained a number of Gnostic writings, providing first hand accounts of their beliefs, and generally confirming what the church fathers had said about them (see next question).

What is the Nag Hammadi Library?

The Nag Hammadi Library is a collection of thirteen codices discovered in Egypt in 1945. A codex is an ancient book, with individual pages written on both sides and bound together. This is different from a scroll, where sheets are pasted or sewn together and rolled up. Dan Brown inaccurately identifies the Nag Hammadi codices as "scrolls" (*DVC,* pp. 234, 245 [254, 266]). The thirteen Nag Hammadi codices contained fifty-two separate writings, written in Coptic, an ancient language of Egypt. Most, but not all, of these writings reflect a Gnostic perspective.[7]

Are the Gnostic Gospels the earliest Christian records?

We have already dealt with this question at some length in our discussion of the canon of Scripture in Chapter 2. While scholars debate the age and provenance (place of composition) of the Gnostic gospels, they are certainly *not* the earliest Christian records. While there is good evidence that *all* of the New Testament documents can be dated to the first century AD, *none* of the Gnostic writings can be confidently dated before the middle of the second century. And most were clearly written much later.

The earliest New Testament documents are the letters of Paul, written in the 50s and 60s of the first century. The letter of James may be even earlier, written around AD 45. Mark's Gospel was probably the first gospel written, in the 50s or 60s of the first century. Matthew and Luke likely followed in the 60s or 70s, and John was probably written last, sometime in the 90s.[8] Quotations and allusions from the four Gospels in the so-called "apostolic fathers" (the generation of church

---

[7] For introductions and English translations of the Nag Hammadi library see J. N. Robinson, ed., *The Nag Hammadi Library in English* (New York: HarperSan-Francisco, 1990).

[8] For evidence of these dates see my forthcoming text, *Four Portraits: One Jesus. An Introduction to Jesus and the Gospels* (Grand Rapids: Zondervan).

leaders after the apostles) confirm their first century date, and there is good evidence that they were circulating as a collection by the early second century.[9] Justin Martyr, in the mid-second century, quotes frequently from them and refers to the four as the "memoirs of the apostles."[10] The Muratorian fragment, a canonical list dating from about AD 160, identifies the four as authoritative Scripture.[11] By the late second century, the fourfold Gospel is so firmly established that Irenaeus argues that there can be neither more nor less than four Gospels, comparing them to the four winds and the four points of the compass.[12]

It is also significant that when Irenaeus writes against various second century heresies, he does not accuse them of producing their own gospels, but of selectively using these four Gospels. The Ebionites used only Matthew; the heretic Marcion edited Luke to suit his purposes; those who separated the humanity of Jesus from the deity of the Christ were using Mark; and the Valentinians favored John's Gospel.[13] This confirms that even these opponents of the orthodox church recognized the antiquity and authority of the four canonical Gospels, and so tried to draw on them to support their own beliefs.

In contrast to the first century dates of the four New Testament Gospels, most experts date the *Gospel of Thomas* – probably the earliest of the Gnostic gospels – to the mid-second century. *Thomas* appears to be dependent on the

---

[9] See Martin Hengel, *The Four Gospels and the One Gospel of Jesus Christ. An investigation of the collection and origin of the canonical Gospels* (Harrisburg, PA: Trinity Press International, 2000). Hengel points out that the early titles given to the four, "according to Mark," "according to Matthew," etc. confirms this.

[10] Justin Martyr, *First Apology* 66, 67; *Dialogue with Trypho,* 100-107.

[11] See Bruce Metzger, *The Canon of the New Testament: Its Origin, Development and Significance* (Oxford: Clarendon, 1987), pp. 191-201.

[12] Irenaeus, *Against Heresies* 3.11.8.

[13] Irenaeus, *Against Heresies* 3.11.7. This point is made by Darrell Bock, *Breaking the Da Vinci Code* (Nashville: Nelson, 2004), pp. 111-113.

canonical Gospels, drawing on them as sources.[14] There are also allusions in *Thomas* to the letters of Paul and other portions of the New Testament.[15] The logical conclusion is that *Thomas* is attempting to reinterpret the teaching of Jesus and the apostles in a Gnostic manner. The two documents that *The Da Vinci Code* refers to with reference to Mary Magdalene are even later than the *Gospel of Thomas*. The *Gospel of Philip* and *Gospel of Mary* were probably written in the late second or third century.

Even if these Gnostic gospels could be shown to be among the earliest Christian documents (which they cannot), *The Da Vinci Code* still gets it wrong, since it misrepresents what they teach – as the next question shows.

Do the Gnostic Gospels reveal a merely human Jesus?

In *The Da Vinci Code,* Teabing says that the documents of the Nag Hammadi library "speak of Christ's ministry in very human terms." This is why "the Vatican, in keeping with their tradition of misinformation, tried very hard to suppress the release of these scrolls" (*DVC,* p. 234 [254]). This is a curious statement, since in fact the opposite is true. The Gnostic literature has a decidedly *docetic* tone, denying the humanity of Jesus at the expense of his deity. (Docetism claimed that Jesus only appeared to be human, when in fact he was pure spirit.) This is because for Gnostics the physical body was a mere shell for the true spiritual self, which longed to escape and return to its heavenly dwelling. Ironically, it is the New Testament Gospels that most strongly stress the humanity of Jesus. Jesus there expresses a range of human emotions, including compassion (Mark 1:41; 6:34),

[14] This point is debated by scholars. See C. M. Tuckett, "Thomas and the Synoptics," *Novum Testamentum* 30 (1988), pp. 132-57; Klyne Snodgrass, "The Gospel of Thomas: A Secondary Gospel," *Second Century* 7 (1989-1990) 19-38.

[15] See Ben Witherington, *The Gospel Code* (Downers Grove, IL: InterVarsity, 2004), pp. 103-104.

indignation (10:41), grief (3:5), amazement (6:6), anger (3:5), and love (10:21). He experiences all forms of human suffering and deprivation, including pain, hunger, thirst, and fatigue.[16] If Constantine wanted to deny the humanity of Jesus, he should have suppressed the New Testament Gospels, not the Gnostic ones!

Was Jesus a Gnostic teacher?

All the evidence says "no." The claim that Jesus was originally a Gnostic simply does not fit his life setting. Jesus was a first century Jew (all scholars agree on this), and his earliest followers were Palestinian Jews. The New Testament Gospels place Jesus accurately in this Jewish world. He moves around in first century settings like Galilee, Capernaum, Jerusalem, and Samaria. He interacts with groups and people we know from first century Palestine: Pharisees, Sadducees, scribes, synagogue officials, tax collectors, a Roman centurion, Pilate, Herod, Caiaphas, etc. He discusses Jewish issues like the interpretation of the Law, the kingdom of God, ceremonial cleanness, dietary laws, disputes about marriage and divorce.[17]

All of these things place Jesus squarely in the Jewish context in which *we know he lived.* The Gnostic literature, by contrast, does not fit this historical context. In these writings Jesus has esoteric conversations with his followers about Gnostic themes and theology, far removed from his Jewish world. This suggests that the Gnostic interpretation of Jesus was a later development that arose under the influence of Greek philosophical thought and a pagan pantheistic worldview.

---

[16] Pain: Mark 8:31; 9:12; Luke 24:15, 46; Heb. 2:10, 18; 5:8; hunger: Matt. 4:2; 21:18; thirst: John 19:28; fatigue: John 4:6.

[17] The few outside sources we have confirm this picture of Jesus found in the Gospels. See, for example, Josephus, *Antiquities* 18.3.3 §§63-64.

Was Gnosticism liberating and feminist?

Here again, *The Da Vinci Code* gets it very wrong. While it is difficult to make generalizations about Gnosticism since the term encompasses a wide range of documents and beliefs, Dan Brown's claims do not really fit any of them. As we have noted previously, Gnosticism was dualistic, viewing the world of matter as evil. Gnostics did not particularly extol women nor feminine characteristics. In fact, the distinction between male and female was viewed by Gnostics as a distortion of humanity, so that females (as well as males) are less than fully human.[18] In a fascinating passage from the *Gospel of Thomas* (which, as we have said, is probably the earliest of the Gnostic gospels), Simon Peter makes the distinctly anti-feminist comment, "Let Mary leave us, for women are not worthy of life." Instead of rebuking Peter, Jesus provides a solution:

> "I myself shall lead her in order to make her male, so that she too may become a living spirit resembling you males. For every woman who will make herself male will enter the kingdom of heaven." (*Gospel of Thomas* 114).

Women must make themselves *male* to enter the kingdom of heaven! This hardly sounds like the Jesus of the New Testament, who honors women as disciples and treats them as

---

[18] Saying 22 of the *Gospel of Thomas* points out that true humanity is a merging of male and female: "When you make the two one...and when you make the male and the female one and the same...then you will enter [the kingdom]." By contrast, the book of Genesis says that God's creation of male and female, as distinct individuals bearing the image of God, is part of his creative design, and pronounces this "very good" (Gen. 1:27, 31). The Gnostics, by contrast, viewed the material world as evil.

equals in the kingdom of God.[19] It is not surprising that Dan Brown never has Teabing quote from this passage, since it would refute his view that Gnosticism extolled the sacred feminine! The passage in fact must be understood within the Gnostic worldview that humans are trapped within material shells and salvation is gained by returning to their true spiritual home. Males were evidently one step closer to this state of spiritual enlightenment, so that females are expected to become males in order to attain salvation.

There is indeed some evidence that women may have served in leadership roles in some Gnostic circles and that this was a point of debate within these groups. Mary's prominent role in documents like the *Gospel of Philip* may partly reflect this ongoing debate (on Mary Magdalene, see Chapters 5 and 6 below). It must be added, however, that these same debates were taking place in the orthodox church, both throughout history and continuing today. To caricature the church as misogynist and oppressive and the Gnostics as feminist and liberating is a distortion of the evidence.

---

[19] See Glen G. Scorgie, *The Journey Back to Eden. Restoring the Creator's Design for Women and Men* (Grand Rapids: Zondervan, 2005), Chapter 6, "Jesus and Women."

Chapter 4

Christianity & the "Sacred Feminine"

The Da Vinci Code adopts the view of some neo-pagan feminist writers that the earliest human religion was a form of paganism that lived in peace and harmony with Nature, practiced egalitarian ideals, and worshipped the supreme Mother Goddess. This religion supposedly honored the sacred feminine because of her life-giving power, and sought a balance between male and female principles – the yin and the yang.

A great struggle took place, according to this view, when hateful male-dominated religions – especially Christianity – sought to destroy this pure Nature worship and to replace it with an oppressive religion where only male gods reigned supreme. Sexual union came to be viewed as the original sin of the Garden of Eden, and Eve was vilified as the cause of humanity's fall. As part of its campaign to suppress the sacred feminine, the church supposedly rounded up and burned all free-thinking and scholarly women as witches – a total of five million in all!

This view not only badly distorts the history of ancient paganism and early Christianity, but it misrepresents Christianity as anti-female and opposed to sex.[1] In fact,

---

[1] The term "paganism" is a general one, referring to any polytheistic or pantheistic religion. The term is usually used today in contrast to the three great monotheistic religions: Judaism, Christianity and Islam (though Islam did not arise until the 7th century). The trait all pagan religions have in common is belief in many gods. The capitalized term Pagan, or Neo-pagan, is sometimes used of the modern Wiccan movement which practices nature and Mother Goddess worship.

Christianity was far more liberating for women than its counterparts in the ancient world. Furthermore, the Bible celebrates the sexual union of husband and wife as a beautiful creation of God. According to Genesis 1-2, Adam is incomplete in himself and full humanity is achieved through the one-flesh union of husband and wife (Gen. 1:27; 2:19-25). The Old Testament *Song of Songs* celebrates the joys of courtship and the sexual relationship between a husband and wife.

The Da Vinci Code claims:

"Those deemed 'witches' by the Church included all female scholars, priestesses, gypsies, mystics, nature lovers, herb gatherers, and any women 'suspiciously attuned to the natural world.'...During three hundred years of witch hunts, the Church burned at the stake an astounding five million women." (*DVC,* p. 125 [134])

"The propaganda and bloodshed had worked...Women, once celebrated as an essential half of spiritual enlightenment, had been banished from the temples of the world....The once hallowed act of Hieros Gamos – the natural sexual union between man and woman through which each became spiritually whole – had been recast as a shameful act." (*DVC,* p. 125 [134-35])

"The days of the goddess were over. The pendulum had swung. Mother Earth had become a man's world, and the gods of destruction and war were taking their toll. The male ego had spent two millennia running unchecked by its female counterpart." (*DVC,* p. 125 [135])

Was the earliest religion an egalitarian celebration of the sacred feminine?

Dan Brown is drawing his ideas here from the modern Wiccan movement, also known as Neo-paganism, which claims that the earliest religion in the West was a peace-loving and egalitarian one involving the worship of two great deities, the Mother Goddess who gives birth to all things, and the Horned (male) God, who died and was resurrected each year.[2] Adherents to this religion were supposedly attuned to nature and celebrated the natural cycles of life. It was only when Indo-European invaders swept through Europe and introduced warrior gods and weapons of war that this Mother Goddess religion was suppressed and went underground.[3]

This claim of an early universal belief in a Mother Goddess has been discredited by archaeologists and historians.[4] Most ancient religions were animistic or polytheistic. Animists believe there are spirits in all physical objects, while polytheists believe in many different gods. Historically, these gods and goddesses were generally localized and had specific domains of power. They ruled the mountains, the forests, or the seas, and controlled war, hunting, love, fertility, harvest, etc. Adherents of polytheism sought to appease these gods to gain favor or protection.

This same diversity characterized the religions of the Roman empire in the first century.[5] Contrary to claims of *The*

---

[2] Charlotte Allen, "The Scholars and the Goddess," *The Atlantic Monthly,* vol. 287, no. 1 (January, 2001), pp. 18-22; available at www.theatlantic.com/cqi-bin/o/issues/2001/01/allen.htm. Allen is citing here from a leading Wiccan book, *The Spiral Dance: A Rebirth of the Ancient Religion of the Great Goddess* (1979), by Starhawk (formerly Miriam Simos), a self described witch.

[3] Allen, "The Scholars and the Goddess."

[4] See especially Philip G. Davis, *Goddess Unmasked: The Rise of Neopagan Feminist Spirituality* (Dallas: Spence, 1998) and Ronald Hutton, *The Triumph of the Moon* (Oxford University Press, 1999).

[5] For religions of the Greco-Roman world, see James Jeffers, *The Greco-Roman World of the New Testament Era* (Downers Grove, IL: InterVarsity, 1999), pp. 89-

Da Vinci Code, sun worship was not the "official" religion of the empire. Rome did not have an official religion, and was generally tolerant of all religions. Some people worshipped the gods of the Greek Pantheon; others, a variety of Roman gods; still others participated in the mystery religions – more recent imports from the East. Emperor worship began with Caesar Augustus, who somewhat reluctantly allowed himself to be worshipped as a god. Emperor worship was subsequently adopted by many Roman emperors and all citizens were required to participate as an act of loyalty to the state.[6]

Jews and Christians were unique in the Roman empire – and viewed with suspicion by many – because they rejected all such gods and believed in the one true God of Israel, the Creator and Sustainer of all things. Because of their loyalty to Rome, the Jews had gained the status of a "legal religion" (*religio licita*) and were exempt from emperor worship. Instead, Jewish priests offered sacrifices to Yahweh on behalf of the emperor at the Jerusalem temple. Christians experienced this same protection as long as Christianity was viewed as a sect of Judaism. As Jews and Christians gradually parted ways, persecution against the Christians increased. This was due, at least in part, to their failure to acknowledge the Roman gods.

"Paganism" was not, then, synonymous with worship of the sacred feminine, but represented a diverse array of gods and belief systems. Furthermore, the primary redemptive ritual of pagan religions was not the *hieros gamos* ("sacred marriage") described in *The Da Vinci Code* but rather animal sacrifices intended to appease the gods.[7] Obviously, such

---

109; John Ferguson, *The Religions of the Roman Empire* (New York: Cornell University Press, 1970); Ramsay MacMullen, *Paganism in the Roman Empire* (New Haven, Conn.: Yale University Press, 1981).

[6] Jeffers, *Greco-Roman World,* pp. 100-103.

[7] Ibid, p. 91.

bloody (and animal-unfriendly!) rituals would not have appealed to Dan Brown's readers nearly as much as sex rites. Nor were these ancient religions egalitarian. In Roman religion, for example, it was normally the male head of the household, the *paterfamilias,* who performed the rituals for the family.[8]

The Da Vinci's Code's praise of goddess worship as honoring of women is also misguided. Goddess worship in the ancient world was more often about exploiting women than extolling their virtues. Fertility rites often revolved around pagan temples where slave prostitutes served at the whim of their male customers. Consider, for example, the temple of the goddess Aphrodite in Corinth, which, in the second century BC, boasted the services of a thousand "sacred prostitutes."[9] This debauched institution hardly constitutes the liberation of women that *The Da Vinci Code* extols.

Did the early Jews worship the sacred feminine?

At one point Langdon claims that even Judaism began as a religion of the sacred feminine. He says:

> Early Jews believed that the Holy of Holies in Solomon's Temple housed not only God but also his powerful female equal, Shekinah. Men seeking spiritual wholeness came to the Temple to visit priestesses – or *hierodules* – with whom they made love and experienced the divine through physical union. The Jewish tetragrammaton YHWH – the sacred name of God – in fact derived from Jehovah, an androgynous physical union between the masculine

---

[8] Jeffers, *Greco-Roman World,* p. 92.

[9] Strabo, *Geography* 8.6.20c. Strabo's claims have been questioned by some, since the Greeks did not generally practice slave prostitution (though it was common in the East). See J. Murphy O'Connor, *St. Paul's Corinth: Texts and Archaeology* (Collegeville, MN: Liturgical Press, 1983), 56-58.

> *Jah* and the pre-Hebraic name for Eve, *Havah* (*DVC*, p. 309 [336]).

This claim is ludicrous. Central to Israel's religion was monotheism – belief in the one true God and the rejection of all other "gods" as idols (Exod. 20:3; Ps. 115). While the nation occasionally lapsed into the idolatry of her neighbors, goddess worship was never a part of Israel's religion, and there were certainly no priestesses or sacred prostitutes in the Jerusalem temple.

The Hebrew term *Shekinah* means "that which dwells" and refers to God's glory or presence in the temple. The term is a late one and does not even appear in the Bible. It was coined by later rabbis and first appeared in the Jewish Mishnah (*c.* AD 200) some eight hundred years after the destruction of Solomon's temple.[10] It certainly never referred to God's female consort.

Equally ludicrous is the claim that YHWH was derived from "Jehovah," combining the masculine *Jah* and a pre-Hebraic name for Eve. The term Jehovah is actually a mispronunciation of the divine name YHWH, which was originally probably pronounced "Yahweh." The Jews came to view this name as so sacred that they would not utter it aloud, replacing it either with the Hebrew *Ha-Shem* ("the Name"), or *Adonai* ("Lord"). The name Jehovah resulted when the vowel points for *Adonai* were misread with the consonants for YHWH.

In any case, the divine name has no connection with male and female deities. Yahweh is the covenant name for God and is associated in Exodus 3:14 with the Hebrew phrase "I AM that I AM," meaning "I am the pre-existent One" or "the Eternal One." Apart from containing two of the same Hebrew

---

[10] See "Shekinah," in *Zondervan Pictorial Encyclopedia of the Bible* (ed. M.C. Tenney; Grand Rapids; Zondervan, 1976), vol. 5, pp. 388-391.

letters, the word has no etymological connection to the name Eve (*chavvah*).

Did the church seek to eradicate the pure religion of the sacred feminine?

This, too, is a twisted view of history. Dan Brown apparently expects his readers to connect three unrelated (and fictional) events into one great conspiracy: (1) a supposed struggle between Peter and Mary Magdalene (1st century AD);[11] (2) the Emperor Constantine's presumed attempts to eradicate paganism (4th century AD); and (3) the burning of millions of witches in the Middle Ages. The chronological jumps taken here are mind boggling. First, Constantine and Peter lived two hundred and fifty years apart. Was it Peter in the mid-first century who challenged Mary and sent her scurrying off to France, or was it Constantine two and a half centuries later who suppressed the pure church of Gnosticism founded upon the sacred feminine? Brown seems to present Peter and Constantine as co-conspirators in the overthrow of the sacred feminine.

In reality, as we shall see (Chapter 6, pp. 74-78), there is no evidence that Mary founded a rival church to that of Peter and the other apostles. All the evidence indicates, rather, that Mary and other women disciples worked side-by-side with Peter and the others to establish the apostolic church. The earliest and the only reliable records of this period – the book of Acts and the New Testament Epistles– reveal no hint of rivalry between Peter and Mary Magdalene. Furthermore, as we have seen, Constantine's actions at the Council of Nicea had nothing to do with either Gnosticism or the sacred feminine. While embracing Christianity, Constantine remained tolerant toward paganism throughout his reign. Finally, the tragic witch burnings of the late Middle Ages did

---

[11] See Chapter 6 for more on this.

not concern millions of victims, nor did they have anything to do with the sacred feminine, goddess worship, or free-thinking women. They were rather the result of an age marked by superstition and hysteria. See the next question for more on this.

Did the church burn five million free-thinking women as witches?

The European period of history dubbed the "Burning Times" has become an important part of the lore of the modern Wiccan movement. Adherents of Neo-paganism claim that during the Middle Ages (5th-14th centuries), the church burned between five to nine million witches in its attempt to destroy this ancient religion of Nature. *The Da Vinci Code* picks up this claim and links it with the imagined struggle between the church and the sacred feminine. Langdon notes that over a period of three centuries, "Those deemed 'witches' by the Church included all female scholars, priestesses, gypsies, mystics, nature lovers, herb gatherers, and any women 'suspiciously attuned to the natural world.'" (*DVC,* p. 125 [134]).

In fact, Dan Brown is depending here on outdated and inaccurate research. In an article on Neo-paganism in *The Atlantic Monthly,* Charlotte Allen sums up current research on the Burning Times:

> Most scholars today believe that the actual number of executions is in the neighborhood of 40,000. The most recent study of historical witchcraft is *Witches and Neighbors* (1996), by Robin Briggs, an historian at Oxford University. Briggs pored over the documents of European witch trials and concluded that most of them took place during the relatively short period, 1550 to 1630, and were largely confined to parts of

> present-day France, Switzerland, and Germany that were already racked by the religious and political turmoil of the Reformation.[12]

Not only has the number of witches killed been wildly exaggerated, but the kind of women involved and the role of the church has also been misrepresented. Allen continues:

> The accused witches, far from including a large number of independent-minded women, were mostly poor and unpopular. Their accusers were typically ordinary citizens (often other women), not clerical or secular authorities. In fact, the authorities generally disliked trying witchcraft cases and acquitted more than half of all defendants. Briggs also discovered that none of the accused witches who were found guilty and put to death had been charged specifically with practicing a pagan religion.[13]

In other words, almost everything that Dan Brown says about the Burning Times is inaccurate. While 40,000 executions is a horrific number and cannot be justified under any circumstances, this is nothing close to the five million claimed in *The Da Vinci Code.* Nor were all of those accused women. Briggs discovered that approximately 20-25 percent were men, debunking the myth that this was a crusade against free-thinking women.

In another recent article, Jenny Gibbons, a self described Neo-pagan, confirms these facts and numbers and calls on her own movement to get its history right. "We Neopagans now face a crisis. As new data appeared, historians altered their theories to account for it. We have not....We owe it to

---

[12] Allen, "The Scholars and the Goddess."
[13] Allen, "The Scholars and the Goddess."

ourselves to study the Great Hunt more honestly, in more detail, and using the best data available."[14]

Was the early church misogynist and oppressive to women?

The New Testament documents, which supposedly were chosen to fit the church's oppressive attitude toward women, in fact give greater status and dignity to women than the society of their day. In the story of Mary and Martha (this is Mary of Bethany, not Mary Magdalene), Jesus praised Mary for taking the role of a disciple, as she sat at his feet learning from him (Luke 10:38-42). This is shocking in a Jewish context where a rabbi would never have a female disciple. A group of female disciples accompanied Jesus and supported his ministry, a practice that would have been counter-cultural in first century Judaism (Luke 8:1-3). Furthermore, if the Gospel writers were misogynist, why would they portray women as the ones who remained faithful to Jesus even at the cross (after the male disciples deserted him!) and as the first witnesses to the resurrection?[15] In a Jewish culture where women were not considered reliable enough to testify in court, the Gospel writers portray them as the foundational witnesses to the Resurrection.

In the book of Acts and the New Testament Epistles, women assume prominent roles as prophets (Acts 21:9), house church leaders (Lydia: Acts 16:13-15), and teachers (Priscilla: Acts 18:26). Paul speaks of various women as his co-workers (Rom. 16:3; Phil. 4:2-3).

Of course, the claim that the church was anti-female also founders on the extraordinary honor given to Mary, the mother of Jesus. The historical veneration of the Virgin Mary

---

[14] Jenny Gibbons, "Recent Developments in the Study of the Great European Witch Hunt"; accessed at www.draeconin.com/database/witchhunt.htm.

[15] At the cross: Matt. 27:55-56; Mark 15:40-41; Luke 23:49; John 19:25-27. Discovery of the empty tomb: Matt. 28:1-10; Mark 16:1-8; Luke 24:1-12; John 20:1-13.

in Roman Catholicism – including claims of her immaculate conception, her sinlessness, her bodily assumption to heaven, and her roles as Mother of God, Co-redemptress with Christ, and Queen of Heaven – rivals anything *The Da Vinci Code* says about Mary Magdalene. Without entering into the debate between Protestants and Roman Catholics on this issue,[16] we simply note that the church was certainly not averse to attributing high status and authority to a woman.[17]

It is certainly true that some limitations are placed on leadership roles for women in certain New Testament texts,[18] and that Jesus chose twelve men to serve as his apostles (Mark 3:13-19). These limitations have been interpreted differently within various Christian traditions. Roman Catholics limit the priesthood to males. Some Protestant denominations ordain women as pastors and elders, while others do not. The church today continues to debate whether the New Testament limitations were intended for specific first century contexts or whether they were meant to apply for all time. But in either case, there is little doubt that the New Testament gives much greater status and dignity to women than ancient society at large. Furthermore, the Bible clearly teaches the full equality of males and females as bearers of the image of God (Gen. 1:27) and as equal heirs of salvation (Gal. 3:28). The claim that the orthodox church transformed Jesus from "the original feminist" into a misogynist simply cannot be sustained.[19]

---

[16] See Norman L. Geisler and Ralph E. MacKenzie, *Roman Catholics and Evangelicals. Agreements and Differences* (Grand Rapids: Baker, 1995), ch. 15.

[17] Some feminists dismiss the Virgin Mary as passive, submissive and sexless, an unworthy model for feminists. This is hardly fair, however. It not only misrepresents Mary, but it imposes unwarranted stereotypes about what makes a woman valuable.

[18] See, for example, 1 Tim. 2:11-14.

[19] It is true that some early church leaders as well as their Jewish predecessors exhibit anti-female attitudes and biases. Sexism and oppression have always been

---

part of the human condition, and it should not surprise us that it surfaces in churches as well as in other human institutions.

CHAPTER 5

JESUS AND MARY MAGDALENE: HUSBAND AND WIFE?

The Da Vinci Code claims that Jesus was married to Mary Magdalene, and that she was pregnant when he was crucified. After his death she bore him a daughter named Sarah, and descendants of their union are alive today. The "evidence" for this marriage is the assertion that it would have been unthinkable for a Jewish rabbi like Jesus to remain single. Furthermore, according to *The Da Vinci Code,* the record of Jesus' marriage to Mary is a firm "part of the historical records," and its "countless references" have been explored *ad nauseam* by modern historians.

In reality, there is *no* ancient evidence for this marital relationship, and nobody even suggested it until the book *Holy Blood, Holy Grail* appeared in the 1980s.

The Da Vinci Code claims:

"...Jesus as a married man makes infinitely more sense than our standard biblical view of Jesus as a bachelor...Because Jesus was a Jew...the social decorum during that time virtually forbid a Jewish man to be unmarried..." (DVC, p. 245 [265]; spoken by Teabing and Langdon)

"... the marriage of Jesus and Mary Magdalene is part of the historical record. ...I shan't bore you with the countless references to Jesus and Magdalene's union. That has been explored ad nauseam by modern historians." (*DVC*, p. 245, 247 [265, 267]; spoken by Teabing)

Was Jesus married?

First, it is fallacious logic to say, as Teabing does, that since most men of Jesus' day were married, therefore Jesus must have been married. Consider the statement, "Most British prime ministers are men; therefore Margaret Thatcher is a man." This is clearly a false syllogism. Although Jewish men of Jesus' day were *usually* married, there were many exceptions. For example, the Essenes of the Dead Sea community at Qumran remained single.[1] The apostle Paul was single, and it appears Barnabas was as well (1 Cor. 7:7; 1 Cor. 9:5-6). In both Judaism and Christianity, singleness and celibacy were esteemed as a means of complete devotion to the Lord.[2] The apostle Paul wrote, "I wish that all men were as I am [that is, unmarried]. But each man has his own gift from God; one has this gift, another has that" (1 Cor. 7:7). Jesus himself taught the legitimacy of celibacy for those able to accept this status (Matt. 19:10-12). It cannot, therefore, be assumed that all Jewish men of Jesus' age were married.

While most *rabbis* were certainly married, Jesus' ministry more closely resembled that of a *prophet.* A rabbi would generally be associated with a local synagogue and would settle down with a wife and children (something like a local pastor). A prophet, on the other hand, might have an itinerant (traveling) ministry and remain single to be totally devoted to the Lord. John the Baptist, the prophet and forerunner of the Messiah, was almost certainly unmarried. It is significant, then, that three of the central figures in the establishment of Christianity – John the Baptist, the apostle Paul, and Jesus himself – all had itinerant ministries and all remained single.

Of course we must also keep in mind the uniqueness of Jesus. Here is a man who devoted himself wholly to God,

---

[1] On the celibacy of the Essenes, see Josephus, *Antiquities* 18.1.5 §20-21; *War* 2.88.2 §§119-121; Philo, *Hypothetica* 11.14-17.

[2] See 1 Cor. 7:32-33; Luke 2:36-37; cf. the apocryphal book of Judith 8:4-8.

who challenged convention at every turn, who called for total commitment from his followers, and who claimed to be God's agent of final salvation. We should not be surprised that he did not live and act like "just another rabbi."

There are, in fact, no ancient references to Jesus' marriage. The Gospels confirm Jesus' singleness in a variety of ways. Jesus said the Son of Man had no place to lay his head (Matt. 8:20; Luke 9:58). If he had a wife, he surely would have provided a home for her. From the cross, Jesus commends his mother to the care of John, but he does not assign any care for a wife – even though Mary Magdalene was present! (John 6:25-27). Most significantly, there is no hint of any sexual or marital relationship between Jesus and the women who supported him. Jesus' opponents mustered every accusation they could against him, including blasphemy, demon possession, drunkenness, and association with sinners.[3] Yet there is no hint of sexual impropriety. If there were any such scandalous rumors, his enemies would surely have raised them against him.

There is also implicit evidence in the Pauline letters for Jesus' singleness. In First Corinthians (written about AD 55), Paul writes, "Don't we have the right to take a believing wife along with us, as do the other apostles and the Lord's brothers and Cephas [= Peter]?" (1 Cor. 9:5). Paul identifies himself as one who has not exercised his legitimate right to take a wife, a right exercised by Jesus' brothers, Peter, and the other apostles. As Ben Witherington points out, "Here Paul certainly would have mentioned the example of Jesus being married had it been so....Paul assumes his audience knows perfectly well that neither he nor Jesus were married."[4]

---

[3] Mark 2:7, 16; 3:22; 14:64; Matt. 11:19.

[4] Ben Witherington, *The Gospel Code* (Downers Grove, IL: InterVarsity, 2004), p. 31.

Do the Gnostic gospels claim Jesus was married to Mary Magdalene?

Actually, no. While the Gnostic gospels describe a special esoteric relationship between Jesus and Mary Magdalene, this relationship is not unique (Jesus has it with other disciples as well), nor is it identified as a *marital* or *sexual* relationship. In *The Da Vinci Code,* Teabing reads from a passage from the Gnostic *Gospel of Philip* that certainly surprises many Christians:

> Teabing pointed to a passage. "The Gospel of Philip is always a good place to start." Sophie read the passage: *And the companion of the Saviour is Mary Magdalene. Christ loved her more than all the disciples and used to kiss her often on her mouth. The rest of the disciples were offended by it and expressed disapproval. They said to him, "Why do you love her more than all of us?"* (*DVC*, p. 246 [266]; quoting from the *Gospel of Philip* 63.33-64.4[5])

Teabing goes on to say that "any Aramaic scholar" will confirm that the word *companion* literally means "spouse." This is simply false. First, the *Gospel of Philip* is not written in Aramaic, but Coptic. Second, the Coptic word used here is derived from the Greek *koinōnos,* which does not "literally" mean spouse. It is a general word for a companion or comrade, and can refer to a variety of relationships. The more common Greek word for "wife" is *gunē,* which is *not* used here. The most likely meaning of "companion" in this context

[5] The text is actually fragmentary and has to be reconstructed. It reads: "And the companion of the [...] Mary Magdalene. [...loved] her more that [all] the disciples [and used to] kiss her [often] on her [...]. The rest of [the disciples...]. They said to him, 'Why do you love her more than all of us?'" See the text in *The Nag Hammadi Library in English* (ed. James M. Robinson; HarperSanFrancisco, 1988), p. 148 (henceforth: *NHL*).

is something like "spiritual sister."[6] Indeed, elsewhere in the Gnostic literature Jesus addresses Mary as "sister."[7]

Still, the passage is certainly startling. Jesus and Mary kissing! Jesus loving Mary more than the other disciples? What's going on here? Several points of clarification are in order:

(1) First, the *Gospel of Philip* was composed in the 3rd century AD and shows dependence on the New Testament Gospels. No scholars – even those sympathetic to Gnosticism – consider this passage to reflect an authentic story about Jesus. It is rather an expression of Gnostic theology placed in the mouth of Mary and other disciples.[8]

(2) Second, we misunderstand Gnosticism if we read into the passage a marital or sexual relationship between Jesus and Mary. As we have seen (pp. 40-41), Gnosticism viewed the material world and the physical body as evil. The goal was to escape the defilement of the flesh and to return to true spiritual knowledge and existence. Far from extolling the "sacred feminine" or sexual freedom, the *Gospel of Philip* elsewhere describes sexual intercourse as carnal and defiling. In his introduction to the standard edition of the text, Wesley Isenberg notes that, according to the *Gospel of Philip*, "'Defiled women' are all women who participate in sexual intercourse, i.e., in 'the marriage of defilement,' which is fleshly and lustful (81,34-82,10)."[9]

(3) The kiss, therefore, is not a sexual one, but a kiss of spiritual fellowship that imparts spiritual knowledge (*gnōsis*)

---

[6] See Witherington. *Gospel Code,* p. 36 for this suggestion.

[7] *Dialogue of the Savior* 132.26 (*NHL,* p. 249).

[8] Karen King, for example, in her introduction to the *Gospel of Mary* in *NHL* says that "The confrontation of Mary with Peter, a scenario also found in *The Gospel of Thomas, Pistis Sophia,* and *The Gospel of the Egyptians,* reflects some of the tensions in second century Christianity. Peter and Andrew represent orthodox positions that deny the validity of esoteric revelation and reject the authority of women to teach" (*NHL,* p. 524).

[9] Wesley W. Isenberg, "The Gospel of Philip," in *NHL,* p. 140.

from Jesus. This is evident elsewhere in the *Gospel of Philip,* where Jesus contrasts those begotten in the material world with those begotten in the spiritual realm: "For it is by a kiss that the perfect conceive and give birth. For this reason we also kiss one another. We receive conception from the grace which is in one another."[10] Notice that they kiss *one another,* confirming that this is not a sexual thing between Jesus and Mary, but it relates to fellowship in the community. This is the kiss of communal fellowship between family and friends so common throughout the Middle East.[11] Notice also that the goal is spiritual conception, which in Gnosticism was achieved through the impartation of secret knowledge. Even Karen King, a strong advocate of the theory that Mary Magdalene's influence was suppressed by the church, acknowledges that the kiss here is asexual – a holy kiss or kiss of fellowship between believers.[12]

Further proof that the kiss is not sexual is found in another Gnostic text, *The (Second) Apocalypse of James.* Here Jesus passes on secret knowledge to his half-brother James by means of a kiss.

> "And he kissed my mouth. He took hold of me, saying, 'My beloved! Behold, I shall reveal to you those (things) that (neither) [the] heavens nor their archons have known.... Behold, I shall reveal to you everything, my beloved.'"[13]

---

[10] *Gospel of Philip* 59.2-5 (*NHL,* p. 145).
[11] See Rom. 16:16; 1 Cor. 16:20; 2 Cor. 13:12; 1 Thess. 5:16; 1 Pet. 5:14.
[12] Karen King, *The Gospel of Mary of Magdala: Jesus and the First Woman Apostle* (Santa Rosa, CA: Polebridge Press, 2003), pp. 145-46. Cf. Esther de Boer, who similarly asserts, "We must not understand this 'kissing' in a sexual sense, but in a spiritual sense. The grace which those who kiss exchange makes them born again" (*Mary Magdalene. Beyond the Myth* [tr. John Bowden; London: SCM, 1997], p. 71).
[13] *2 Apoc. James* 56.14-57.9 (*NHL,* p. 274).

Notice that not only does Jesus kiss his brother James just like he kissed Mary, but he refers to him as "my beloved." If this passage were about Mary Magdalene, it would surely have been quoted in *The Da Vinci Code* as proof positive that Jesus and Mary were married! In fact we completely misread these Gnostic texts if we impose sexual or marital categories on them. Jesus' brother James receives special status because Jesus has passed on secret knowledge to him, not because they have a sexual or marital relationship. Mary Magdalene plays a similar role in the *Gospel of Philip* and the *Gospel of Mary*.

But what about the apparent jealously expressed by the disciples in the *Gospel of Philip*? On the one hand, this confirms again that the passage is not about a sexual relationship. Why would the disciples be jealous because Jesus kissed his wife? The explanation rather lies in the relationship between the Gnostics who produced these texts and the larger Christian community. The second century Gnostics were engaged in fierce competition with the orthodox church. The early Christians honored the teachings of the apostles recorded in the New Testament Gospels and the Epistles. The Gnostics rejected much of this teaching and asserted that *they* were the true heirs of the secret *gnōsis* ("knowledge") passed down by Jesus – knowledge that enabled them to gain true spiritual enlightenment. Their own writings claim to be secret revelations transmitted apart from orthodox channels to disciples like Mary, Thomas, Philip, etc. Like the *Gospel of Philip*, the late second century *Gospel of Mary Magdalene* presents Mary as a true recipient of Jesus' teaching. In the following passage, Mary has just shared a vision from Jesus that is clearly Gnostic in flavor. Andrew and Peter (representing the orthodox church) respond:

> But Andrew answered and said to the brethren, "Say what you (wish to) say about what she has said. I at least do not believe that the Savior said this. For certainly these teachings are strange ideas." Peter answered and spoke concerning these same things. He questioned them about the Savior: "Did he really speak with a woman without our knowledge (and) not openly? Are we to turn about and all listen to her? Did he prefer her to us?"[14]

Mary then speaks up to defend her revelation and is defended in turn by another disciple, Levi:

> Then Mary wept and said to Peter, "My brother Peter, what do you think? Do you think that I thought this up myself in my heart, or that I am lying about the Savior?" Levi answered and said to Peter, "Peter, you have always been hot-tempered. I see you contending against the women like the adversaries. But if the Savior made her worthy, who are you indeed to reject her? Surely the Savior knows her very well. That is why he loved her more than us."[15]

It should first be noted that this text was written, at the earliest, in the late second century. Like *Philip,* it has no legitimate claim to being an authentic historical dialogue between Mary and Peter. Rather, these later Gnostic writings were composed to defend the antiquity and authority of Gnostic teachings over against the teachings of the orthodox church. Mary, representing the Gnostic position, claims special secret knowledge from Jesus that Peter and Andrew, representing the orthodox church, were not privy to. Levi,

---

[14] *Gospel of Mary* 17.10-20 (*NHL,* p. 526).
[15] *Gospel of Mary* 18.1-14 (*NHL,* pp. 526-27).

representing the voice of reason, points out that Peter has always been hot-headed and over-reactionary and that he needs to calm down and listen to Mary. He then acknowledges that Mary did have a special relationship with Jesus and so perhaps her new revelations are true. The passage has nothing to do with a marital or sexual relationship between Jesus and Mary. It is rather a claim to authority for Gnostic teaching.

We must conclude, therefore, that there are no ancient sources, not even the *Gospel of Philip* or the *Gospel of Mary,* which claim that Jesus was married or had a sexual relationship with Mary Magdalene. When Teabing says, "I shan't bore you with the countless references to Jesus and Magdalene's union" (*DVC,* p. 247 [267]), the reason he "shan't bore them" is because there aren't any! The claim of this royal bloodline of Jesus is a modern invention, promoted in sensationalistic books like *Holy Blood, Holy Grail*[16] by Michael Baigent, Richard Leigh and Henry Lincoln and *The Woman with the Alabaster Jar*[17] by Margaret Starbird. None of these authors is either an historian or a biblical scholar. To claim that Jesus' marriage to Mary Magdalene is "part of the historical record" is tabloid journalism rather than sound historical research.

If Jesus were married and had children, would this undermine the truth of Christianity?

This is the premise behind *The Da Vinci Code's* claim that the church *had to suppress* the marriage and family of Jesus. Teabing says, "A child of Jesus would undermine the critical notion of Christ's divinity and therefore the Christian

---

[16] Michael Baigent, Richard Leigh and Henry Lincoln, *Holy Blood, Holy Grai* (New York: Dell, 1983).

[17] Margaret Starbird, *The Woman with the Alabaster Jar* (Rochester, VT: Bear, 1993).

Church" (*DVC,* 254 [274]). But the Bible teaches that Jesus was fully human as well as fully divine,[18] and marriage and procreation are a natural part of human life. There is nothing evil or sinful about sexual relations. The idea that sex is evil or defiling is a Gnostic idea, not a Christian one! God created sex as a means of procreation and as a wonderful expression of love between a husband and wife (Gen. 2:24).

It is certainly true that some later church leaders denigrated marriage and viewed the celibate life as a higher calling, but this was not the teaching of Jesus or the apostles. Jesus himself affirmed the institution of marriage and the "one flesh" sexual union of husband and wife (Mark 10:7-8). As noted above (p. 63), Peter and other apostles were married, as were Jesus' brothers who were leaders in the church (1 Cor. 9:5). While Paul extols the single life as a means to unencumbered ministry for the Lord, he also affirms marriage as an equally high calling (1 Cor. 7). So there is no reason Jesus could not have been married and had normal sexual relations. But, as we have seen, there is not a shred of evidence that he was in fact married (pp. 62-69). Jesus no doubt recognized that the responsibilities of marriage and family would distract him from the messianic task that God had entrusted to him.

[18] See John 1:1, 14; Heb. 1:1-3; 2:17.

CHAPTER 6

THE REAL MARY MAGDALENE: FAITHFUL DISCIPLE, PROSTITUTE, OR HOLY GRAIL?

The Da Vinci Code claims that Mary was not only the wife of Jesus but also his chosen successor. As a descendant of the royal line of Benjamin, Mary's marriage to Jesus would have merged the royal lines of Benjamin and Judah and created a powerful Jewish dynasty. Peter, however, was a sexist disciple who jealously opposed Mary and sought to discredit her before the rest of the disciples. The church, which was misogynist and patriarchal, took Peter's side, repudiating Mary's leadership role and transforming her into a sordid prostitute. In this way they removed Mary's rightful place as the cofounder of Christianity and suppressed Jesus' teaching concerning goddess worship and the sacred feminine.

The book further claims that under persecution from the church, Mary fled to France with her daughter Sarah, where she found refuge with the Jewish community. Her descendants founded the Merovingian dynasty of French kings, through whom her lineage continues today. Although traditionally the "Holy Grail" has been understood as the cup or chalice that Jesus drank from at the Last Supper, *The Da Vinci Code* claims the Grail is Mary herself, who carried Jesus' child in her womb.

While *The Da Vinci Code* gets almost every fact about Mary wrong, it is certainly true that she is one of the more misunderstood women in the Bible. *Who, in fact, was she?*

The Da Vinci Code claims:

"That unfortunate misconception [that Mary was a prostitute] is the legacy of a smear campaign launched by the early Church. The Church needed to defame Mary Magdalene in order to cover up her dangerous secret – her role as the Holy Grail." (*DVC,* p. 244 [264]; spoken by Teabing)

"According to these unaltered gospels, it was not *Peter* to whom Christ gave directions with which to establish the Christian Church, It was *Mary Magdalene."* (*DVC,* p. 248 [268]; spoken by Teabing)

"Mary Magdalene was of royal descent...By marrying into the powerful House of Benjamin, Jesus fused two royal bloodlines, creating a potent political union with the potential of making a legitimate claim to the throne and restoring the line of kings as it was under Solomon...The legend of the Holy Grail is a legend about royal blood." (*DVC,* p. 249 [269-270]; spoken by Teabing)

"Behold," Teabing proclaimed, "the greatest cover-up in human history. Not only was Jesus Christ married, but He was a father. My dear, Mary Magdalene was the Holy Vessel. She was the chalice that bore the royal bloodline of Jesus Christ." (*DVC,* p. 249 [270]; spoken by Teabing)

Was Mary Magdalene a prostitute?

No, there is no evidence that Mary was a prostitute. Here *The Da Vinci Code* (p. 244 [264]) actually gets it right while many in the church have gotten it wrong. The identification of Mary as a prostitute did not result from sinister motives of the church to discredit her (see next question), but rather from confusion in the church concerning at least four different women in the Gospels. These women were:

(1) Mary Magdalene, one of Jesus' female disciples;[1]

(2) Mary of Bethany, sister of Martha and Lazarus, who was both a disciple of Jesus and one of the women who anointed his feet;[2]

(3) an unnamed woman with a sinful reputation who also anointed Jesus' feet (Luke 7:36-50);

(4) another unnamed woman accused of committing adultery and brought before Jesus in an attempt to trap him (John 7:53-8:11).[3]

Because of the confusion concerning these different women and events, Pope Gregory the Great, in a late sixth century sermon, declared all four of them to be the same woman.[4] The reasoning goes like this: Since Mary Magdalene is first mentioned a few verses after the account of the notorious sinful woman who anointed Jesus' feet (Luke 7:36-50; 8:2), the two must be one and the same. Since Mary of Bethany shares the same name as the former and anointed Jesus' feet like the latter (John 12:1-8),[5] the three now become one. Finally, Jesus' forgiveness of Mary's sin is discovered by linking her with the woman caught in adultery (John 7:53). What were originally four different women have now morphed into one!

---

[1] Matt. 27:56, 61; 28:1; Mark 15:40, 47; 16:1; Luke 8:2; 24:10; John 19:25; 20:1-18.

[2] Luke 10:38-42; John 11:1-44; 12:1-8; cf. Matt. 26:6-13 and Mark 14:3-9, where an anointing is described, but Mary is not named.

[3] This last passage is textually questionable and probably not an original part of John's Gospel. It seems likely, however, that it was an authentic tradition about Jesus passed down in the early church. See B. Metzger, *A Textual Commentary on the Greek New Testament* (2nd ed. Stuttgart: United Bible Societies, 1994), pp. 187-189.

[4] In the sermon, probably delivered in AD 591, Gregory said "She whom Luke calls the sinful woman, whom John calls Mary, we believe to be the Mary from whom seven devils were ejected according to Mark" (Homily 33, in *Homiliarum in evangelia*, Lib. II, *Patrologia Latina*, vol. 76 [Paris: J.-P. Migne, 1844-1864], col. 1239).

[5] Cf. Matt. 26:6-13; Mark 14:3-9.

The unfortunate result of this confusion is that Mary Magdalene came to be viewed in the church as a repentant prostitute. The error was finally corrected by the Roman Catholic Church in 1969 when it changed its liturgical calendar,[6] but Mary's role as a prostitute was too firmly imbedded in the public's imagination for this to make much difference. Countless sermons have been preached on her as a repentant sinner. In the eighteenth century *Magdalen houses* and *Magdalen laundries* were established as places of reform for prostitutes and women who bore children out of wedlock. Almost every movie made about Jesus, including such diverse portrayals as *Jesus Christ Superstar, The Last Temptation of Christ,* and *The Passion of the Christ,* has mistakenly identified Mary as a prostitute.

If Mary Magdalene wasn't a prostitute, who was she?

The New Testament Gospels provide us with the only early and reliable evidence about Mary. "Magdalene" probably means "from Magdala," referring to Mary's hometown, a village on the west side of the Sea of Galilee (Luke 8:2).[7] Because Mary (or Miriam) was a very common name in the first century, the various Marys in the New Testament are generally identified by a descriptive phrase, usually related to parental or spousal relationship: "Mary the mother of Jesus" (Acts 1:4), "Mary the wife of Clopas" (John 19:25), "Mary the mother of James" (Matt. 27:56). The fact that Mary Magdalene is not named with reference to a husband may imply she was either single or a widow.

---

[6] See Katherine L. Jansen, *The Making of the Magdalen: Preaching and Popular Devotion in the Later Middle Ages* (Princeton, NJ: Princeton University Press, 2000), pp. 34-35.

[7] Magdala is never mentioned in the New Testament (except in a variant reading at Matt. 15:39), but the Jewish Talmud identifies the village as about a twenty minutes walk from Tiberias (BDAG, p. 608).

From the Gospels we learn only a few basic facts about Mary:

(1) She was one of the women disciples who supported Jesus during his ministry in Galilee (Luke 8:1-3; cf. Mark 15:41). This service has sometimes been treated as merely domestic duties like providing meals, but Luke 8:3 makes it clear it included financial support. The implication is that these were influential upper class women who had been attracted to Jesus' message and ministry and so helped to support him. One of the women, Joanna, is identified as the wife of Chuza, King Herod's household manager, a position of significant social status and influence. Though Mary is not singled out as having either wealth or influence, the assumption seems to be that she, like these other women, had the means to support Jesus.

(2) Luke also tells us that Jesus exorcized seven demons from Mary (Luke 8:2; cf. Mark 16:9). Though the circumstance of this exorcism is never described, it is clear that prior to meeting Jesus, Mary was a very disturbed woman. This may help to explain her (apparent) singleness. Gratitude for his healing touch is likely what prompted Mary to follow Jesus in discipleship.

(3) Mary was present with other women at the climactic events in Jesus' ministry: his crucifixion,[8] his burial,[9] and at the discovery of his empty tomb.[10] Though the male disciples fled in terror, the women remained faithful to Jesus at the cross.

(4) In an important episode in John's Gospel, Mary encounters Jesus alone at the empty tomb, and serves as the first witness to the resurrected Lord (John 20:1-2, 10-18).

---

[8] Mark 15:40; Matt. 27:56; John 19:25.
[9] Mark 16:1; Matt. 27:61.
[10] Mark 15:47; Matt. 28:1; Luke 24:10.

Despite these relatively few references, we should not downplay or denigrate Mary's importance. She must have been a significant follower of Jesus since she is almost always listed first among the women disciples, just as Peter is among the Twelve.[11] This suggests that she was one of the most prominent of Jesus' women disciples. This is reinforced by the fact that she was granted the privilege to be the first to witness the resurrected Christ.

Unfortunately, after the Gospel resurrection accounts, Mary disappears from the historical record. This is not surprising, of course, since it is true of almost every other New Testament character. Like many others, Mary only reappears centuries later in legends told about her. But these have no real claim to authenticity (see pp. 85-87 below).

Did the church demote Mary?

So did the church seek to discredit Mary's role as Jesus' wife and successor by making her into a prostitute, as *The Da Vinci Code* claims? In fact, the truth is not nearly so scandalous or sensationalistic. As noted above, Mary's inaccurate characterization as a prostitute arose from confusion in the church concerning various women and events. There is no historical evidence for more sinister motives to discredit her leadership. In fact, orthodox leaders in the church spoke highly of Mary and her prominence rose in the church through the centuries. She became a saint; a feast day was established in her honor (July 22), and an entire mass was dedicated to her.[12] All this hardly constitutes a smear campaign.

---

[11] The only exception is John 19:25, where she is listed last among four women.
[12] Carl E. Olson and Sandra Miesel, *The Da Vinci Hoax. Exposing the Errors in* The Da Vinci Code (San Francisco: Ignatius Press, 2004), pp. 87-88. For details, see Jansen, *Making of the Magdalen*, pp. 33-36.

Furthermore, if, as *The Da Vinci Code* claims, "the Church outlawed speaking of the shunned Mary Magdalene" (p. 261 [281]) and radically altered the Bible to suit its own political agenda (p. 231 [250-51]), why does Mary play such a prominent role in the Gospels? Not only is she named first in lists of women followers, but, as noted above, she figures prominently as the first witness to the resurrection.[13] If the church wanted to destroy her reputation, it could have done a much better job of it! There is no evidence that the church demoted Mary from a position of authority or that Jesus intended her to have a more prominent role than the New Testament attributes to her.

The view that Mary was shunned by the orthodox church actually comes from two very different sources. The first are the fanciful legends in conspiracy books like *The Da Vinci Code* and *Holy Blood, Holy Grail,* where Mary is a portrayed as a royal Benjamite princess and the true Holy Grail. We will deal with these claims, which no real scholar takes seriously, in two questions below. A second trajectory, however, is found in the more serious scholarship of feminist authors like Karen King, Susan Haskins and Ann Graham Brock.[14] These scholars find evidence for Mary's original high position in (1) her prominent role in the Gnostic gospels as a channel for Jesus' revelations, (2) the identification of Mary as the "apostle to the apostles" in some early Christian writers, and (3) supposed church evidence for the elevation of Peter at Mary's expense.

---

[13] See the excellent discussion in Olson and Miesel, *The Da Vinci Hoax,* 78-89.

[14] Karen King, *The Gospel of Mary of Magdala: Jesus and the First Woman Apostle* (Santa Rosa, CA: Polebridge Press, 2003); Susan Haskins, *Mary Magdalen: Myth and Metaphor* (New York: Harcourt Brace & Co., 1993); Ann Graham Brock, *Mary Magdalene, The First Apostle: The Struggle for Authority* (Harvard Theological Studies 51; Cambridge, MA: Harvard University Press, 2003).

We have already discussed the first point, noting that Mary's role as a channel for Jesus' revelation is part of the Gnostic claim to esoteric wisdom unavailable through the orthodox church (see pp. 67-69 above). But what about the claim that Mary was an apostle, even *the* preeminent apostle? The identification of Mary as "apostle to the apostles" is often attributed to Hippolytus (c. AD 170-236), second century bishop of Rome, in his commentary on the Song of Songs. As Darrell Bock points out, however, Hippolytus does not single out Mary, but rather he refers to all the women who discovered the empty tomb as apostles.[15] The passage reads:

> Lest the female apostles doubt the angels, Christ himself came to them so that the women would be apostles of Christ and by their obedience rectify the sin of Eve....Christ showed himself to the (male) apostles and said to them:... "It is I who appeared to these women and I who wanted to send them to you as apostles."[16]

The women were apostles, Hippolytus says, because they were "sent" (the meaning of the Greek word *apostolos*) to bear testimony to the resurrection. The term "apostle" in the New Testament is a flexible one. It sometimes refers exclusively to the Twelve appointed by Jesus during his public ministry (Mark 3:14). Other times it refers more generally to those commissioned by the resurrected Lord to spread the good news, like the apostle Paul (Rom. 1:1) and even Barnabas (Acts 14:14). While it is debated today whether women were ever identified as apostles in this sense

---

[15] Darrell Bock, *Breaking the Da Vinci Code* (Nashville: Nelson, 2004), pp. 20, 143-144.

[16] Hippolytus *De Cantico,* 24-26; cited by Brock, *Mary Magdalene, the First Apostle,* pp. 1-2.

(Junia may be called an apostle in Rom. 16:7), Mary Magdalene is never given this title in the New Testament, and there is no evidence that she functioned as an apostle in the first century church. It was only much later, in the Middle Ages, that Mary is singled out as *the* "apostle to the apostles." Even here, however, the title apparently was intended to play on the fact that Mary was "sent" by Jesus to bear witness of the resurrection to the other apostles (John 20:17). This conclusion is in no way meant to downplay Mary's important role as witness to the resurrection, but these scant references can hardly be used to prove that she was *the true successor* to Jesus.

Concerning the third point, Anne Graham Brock claims that there is evidence in the resurrection narratives that Mary's role is being diminished and Peter's is being enhanced: (1) In John's Gospel Jesus appears uniquely to Mary Magdalene at the tomb and gives her a commission to announce the resurrection; (2) in Matthew, Jesus appears to Mary and the other women and gives them a similar commission; (3) in Luke, however, while two angels announce the resurrection to the women, Jesus does not appear to them, and no commission is given. This, Brock argues, shows that Luke is intentionally downplaying the role of Mary.[17]

This is extremely shaky evidence for such a claim. The four Gospels each present a unique perspective on the resurrection, and there is little evidence that Luke is intentionally disparaging Mary. On the contrary, Luke alone identifies Mary Magdalene as one of the prominent woman who financially supported Jesus' ministry (Luke 8:2-3). Scholars have long recognized that Luke shows greater concern for women than the other Gospel writers and seems to intentionally *elevate* their status. Luke, for example,

---

[17] Brock, *Mary Magdalene, the First Apostle,* chs. 2-4.

recounts the episode where another Mary (of Bethany) sits at Jesus' feet and learns from him as a disciple – a remarkable position for a woman in first century Judaism (Luke 10:38-42). The prominent role Peter has in Luke's Gospel is little different from the role he has in the other Gospels, and serves to prepare the reader for Luke's second volume, the book of Acts, where Peter will play an instrumental role in the establishment of the church (Acts 1-5, 10-12). Peter is given an equally important role in Matthew's Gospel, where Jesus entrusts to him the authoritative "keys of the kingdom" (Matt. 16:17-20).

In any case, the evidence from the resurrection narratives is overblown by Brock. In Luke, Mary Magdalene (listed first as usual!) and the other women are given an implicit commission by the angels, and they do proclaim the resurrection "to the eleven [disciples] and to all the rest" (Luke 24:9). It is in fact *the male disciples* who are made to look bad, since "these words [of the women] seemed to them an idle tale, and they did not believe them" (24:10-11). While the women faithfully proclaim the resurrection, it is the men who are (at first) unbelieving! This hardly reveals that Luke is intentionally diminishing Mary's role.

In summary, there is little evidence for the suppression of Mary or the other women in the four canonical Gospels. On the contrary, women are given a more prominent role and status in the Gospels than elsewhere in first century Judaism. Mary Magdalene, far from being a persecuted and marginalized outcast, is presented as a prominent female disciple who is granted the high privilege of being the first witness to the resurrection of Jesus. This does not look much like a smear campaign launched by an evil and misogynist church.

Was Mary Magdalene from the royal house of Benjamin?

Having dealt with the more scholarly claims related to Mary, we turn to the more ludicrous ones. *The Da Vinci Code* makes the odd claim that Mary Magdalene was from the "royal house of Benjamin" and that her marriage to Jesus would have merged two great Jewish dynasties (*DVC,* p. 249 [270]).

First, there is no evidence that Mary Magdalene was from the tribe of Benjamin. Her tribal identity is never mentioned in any ancient sources. While there are some very late medieval legends that Mary had royal ancestry, these do not connect her with the tribe of Benjamin.[18]

Even if Mary could be shown to be a Benjamite, this would mean nothing. There was no "royal house of Benjamin" with a claim to the throne of Israel. Although Saul, the first king of Israel, was from the tribe of Benjamin, no dynasty was established after him (Saul's son Jonathan was killed in battle), and there was never a Jewish tradition of a royal Benjamite line. *The Da Vinci Code's* claim – borrowed from *Holy Blood, Holy Grail*[19] – that merging the royal tribes of Benjamin and Judah would somehow make a powerful royal alliance, is nonsense. The legitimate king of Israel was to be from the tribe of Judah and the royal line of David, Israel's greatest king. When the kingdom of Israel divided after the death of David's son Solomon, Davidic kings continued to reign in the southern kingdom of Judah while several different dynasties ruled in the northern kingdom of Israel. But none of these northern dynasties were led by Benjamites. The tribe of Benjamin was rather allied with Judah in the south. When the prophets spoke of a coming king who would unify the twelve tribes of Israel and reign in justice and righteousness, this king (the Messiah) was

[18] Jansen, *Making of the Magdalen,* p. 149.
[19] Baigent, Leigh, and Lincoln, *Holy Blood, Holy Grail,* p. 347.

always identified as a descendant of David from the tribe of Judah. He was never associated with the tribe of Benjamin.

Was Mary Magdalene the real "Holy Grail"?

The Da Vinci Code calls the Holy Grail "the most enduring legend of all time" (p. 249 [270]). This is hardly the case. The first Grail legends did not appear until the twelfth century AD, eleven hundred years after Christ. Most Grail stories were written between AD 1180 and 1240 and were closely related to the King Arthur legends.[20] The majority were written in French, though some are in German, English, Norwegian, Italian and Portuguese.[21]

The word "grail" comes from the medieval Latin word *gradale,* which meant a dish or bowl. This became in Old French *graal, greal,* or *greel,* from which we get the English *grail.* The first literary reference to the Grail appears in *Perceval,* an unfinished poem written around AD 1170 by Chrétien de Troyes. The story is about a naïve youth's quest to become a knight. The *graal* there is a large bejeweled dish, which is carried by a beautiful woman into a banquet hall during a procession. A silver plate and a bloody lance are also part of the procession. No explanation for these objects is given in the original poem, but later authors adapted and expanded the story. In the many legends that follow, the lance is identified as the one used by a Roman soldier to pierced Jesus' side on the cross, and the Grail is variously identified as (1) the dish from which Jesus ate the Passover lamb, (2) the cup Joseph of Arimathea used to catch the blood of Christ

---

[20] The best recent historical study of the Grail is Roger S. Loomis, *The Grail: From Celtic Myth to Christian Symbol* (Princeton, N. J.: Princeton University Press, new ed., 1993). For a good summary see H.C. Gardiner and J. Misrahi, "Holy Grail, the" in *New Catholic Encyclopedia* (Palatine, IL: Jack Heraty & Associates, 1967), vol. VII, pp. 71-73. The best discussion in *Da Vinci Code* related books is Olson and Miesel, *Da Vinci Hoax,* 178-193.

[21] Gardiner and Misrahi, "Holy Grail," pp. 71-72.

at the cross, (3) the chalice Jesus used at the Last Supper, and (4) a cup or platter that miraculously sustained Joseph of Arimathea with food during an imprisonment. Sometimes these are mixed and merged in a variety of combinations. In one legend, that of Wolfram von Eschenbach (*c.* 1210), the Grail is not a container at all, but a precious stone possessing miraculous powers.[22] Significantly, the Grail is never identified as a person, and certainly not with Mary Magdalene. This is a modern invention.

In the late Middle Ages, Sir Thomas Malory (*Le Morte d'Arthur* [1470]), made a play on words by explaining *san greal* ("holy grail") as *sang real* ("royal blood"). *The Da Vinci Code* makes a great deal of this, claiming that "in its most ancient form, the word *San Greal* was divided in a different spot...Sang Real...*Royal Blood"* (*DVC,* p. 250 [271]). The Sang Real is therefore Jesus' royal offspring through Mary. This claim is silly for several reasons: (1) In Latin and French, royal blood would be *sang royal,* not *sang real. Real* means "royal" in Spanish, but not in Latin or French.[23] (2) The earliest texts speak simply of a "grail," not the "Holy Grail," rendering the etymology irrelevant.[24] (3) The reference to royal blood in the late medieval literature is clearly to Jesus' kingly or messianic blood that paid the penalty for sins, not to his offspring. Malory makes this explicit, identifying "the Sankgreal" as "the blessed bloode of our Lorde Jhesu Cryste."[25]

The other key argument in *The Da Vinci Code* to support the claim that Mary is the Holy Grail is the absence of a chalice in front of Jesus in Leonardo's *The Last Supper* (which we will discuss in the next chapter). This is no real

[22] Gardiner and Misrahi, "Holy Grail," pp. 71-73.
[23] "Royal" in Latin is *royal, regalis,* or *regius.*
[24] Olson and Miesel, *Da Vinci Hoax,* p. 183.
[25] Cited by Loomis, *The Grail,* p. 25.

argument, however, since the Gospels never speak of a large bejeweled chalice, but only of the "cup" that Jesus passed to his disciples at the Passover celebration during which he established the Lord's Supper (the Eucharist). There is no reason to suppose this would have been anything but a normal cup, and in Leonardo's painting, there are cups in front of Jesus and the disciples. The Grail is only missing if one expects to see something from medieval lore rather than from the Bible itself.

The Da Vinci Code also claims that the chalice, represented by a "V" icon (signifying the womb), was the original symbol for femininity, womanhood, and fertility, while the blade, its inverse, represented masculinity. The Grail legend, then, is really an allegory related to Mary Magdalene and the sacred feminine (*DVC,* pp. 237-38, 244 [258, 264]). This claim, too, has no basis in fact. There are different symbols for women and femininity in various cultures, but the so-called chalice does not seem to be one of them. It is certainly not "the original" or universal icon for femininity. The "Λ" and "V" symbols that *The Da Vince Code* calls "blade" and "chalice" are actually two types of chevrons, a symbol that has historically been related to military and heraldic contexts.[26] They do not have uniquely masculine or feminine significance.

In summary, the legends of the Holy Grail did not arise until the late Middle Ages, more than a thousand years after Christ, and even then they were never linked to Mary or to the sacred feminine. The claim that Mary Magdalene is the Holy Grail hangs by a thread of dubious evidence.

---

[26] See Richard Abanes, *The Truth Behind the Da Vinci Code: A Challenging Response to the Bestselling Novel* (Harvest House Publishers, 2004), pp. 47-48, who references the website on symbols of Craig G. Liungman, www.symbols.com. Olson and Miesel (*Da Vinci Hoax,* p. 180) claim Dan Brown takes his theory of the chalice from Riane Eisler, *The Chalice and the Blade* (San Francisco: Harper & Row, 1988).

Are any later traditions about Mary Magdalene true?

According to *The Da Vinci Code,* Mary Magdalene fled to France after Jesus' crucifixion, where she found safe refuge with the Jewish community there and gave birth to her daughter Sarah. According to Teabing, these facts were "scrutinously [*sic*] chronicled by their Jewish benefactors" because "the Jews in France considered Magdalene sacred royalty and revered her as the progenitor of the royal line of kings." He goes on to say that "Countless scholars of that era chronicled Mary Magdalene's days in France, including the birth of Sarah and the subsequent family tree" (*DVC,* p. 255 [276]). Who are these "countless scholars"? Is there any truth in any of this?

The simple answer is no. As we have noted above, we have no reliable historical information concerning Mary Magdalene beyond the few statements made about her in the first century Gospels. Later Christians, however, were not content with this silence, and many legends developed around her life.[27] This is not surprising, of course, since legends arose around almost every character in the Bible. Yet Mary's (undeserved!) reputation as a reformed prostitute, as well as her unique experience of Jesus' resurrection, proved particularly fruitful ground for later myth-makers.

The earliest of these legends come from the 6th century, when Gregory of Tours mentions a tradition that Mary went to Ephesus in Asia Minor (modern Turkey). A tomb thought to be hers was revered there. Modestus, a ruler of Jerusalem

---

[27] On the many later legends related to Mary, see Jansen, *Making of the Magdalen, passim;* Haskins, *Mary Magdalen, passim;* Jane Schaberg, *The Resurrection of Mary Magdalene: Legends, Apocrypha and the Christian Testament* (New York: Continuum, 2002); Lesa Bellevie, *The Complete Idiot's Guide to Mary Magdalene* (New York: Penguin, 2005).

in the 7th century, describes Mary's death in Ephesus as a martyr.[28]

The most famous legends about Mary – and the ones Dan Brown borrows from – began appearing in the eleventh century (a thousand years after she lived!). These claimed that Mary and others set sail from Palestine and arrived in Gaul (France), where Mary preached the gospel and converted many people. In the thirteenth century, *The Golden Legend* by Jacobus de Voragine combined many of the previous legends about Mary's life. In this version Mary travels to France with Martha, Lazarus, and several others. After preaching and performing many miracles, she retires to a life of solitude, fasting and praying for thirty years.[29] The legend reveals its mythological nature by confusing Mary Magdalene with Mary of Bethany, the sister of Martha and Lazarus.

To appreciate the importance of these legends for Christians in the Middle Ages, the so-called "relics trade" must be understood. Interest in saints like Mary Magdalene centered especially around their "relics," which could be objects associated with the saint (like a robe or staff), but more often were their supposed remains, either the corpse or parts of the corpse. These relics were deemed holy and believed to bring healing to those who came near them. For a church to possess such relics brought fame, pilgrims, and the financial benefits that came with these "tourists." Churches often made competing claims to a saint's remains, and the competition could be ruthless. Between the eleventh and thirteenth centuries, two different churches – the abbey at Vézelay and the Provence church of Saint-Maximin – feuded over Mary Magdalene, each claiming to possess her remains.

---

[28] Haskins, *Mary Magdalen,* pp. 106-108; Bellevie, *Mary Magdalene,* p. 126.

[29] See Bellevie, *Mary Magdalene,* pp. 128-29; Haskins, *Mary Magdalen,* pp. 222-226. *The Golden Legend* can be accessed online at www.fordham.edu/halsall/basis/goldenlegend/. The section on Mary Magdalene is in volume 4.

While the intrigues related to these two churches are the most famous, they weren't the only ones to claim a piece of Mary. Tallying the parts of her body that turned up in different places during the Middle Ages, Lesa Bellevie notes that the poor woman left behind at least five full corpses, eight arms, a jawbone, a breastbone, several fingers, several teeth, and an untold amount of hair![30]

Of course no scholar takes these legends seriously. The simple fact is we don't know what happened to Mary after the New Testament period. But even if these legends were true, they still mention nothing about most the claims Dan Brown makes about Mary Magdalene, including (1) her marriage to Jesus, (2) the birth of a daughter named Sarah, (3) her refuge with the Jewish community in France, (4) her establishment of the Merovingian line of kings, or (5) anything about her connection to the Priory of Sion or the Knights Templar. If the medieval legends about Mary have no basis in historical fact, the claims of *The Da Vinci Code* have even less.

---

[30] Bellevie, *Mary Magdalene,* p. 133.

CHAPTER 7

LEONARDO DA VINCI & THE LAST SUPPER

The Da Vinci Code claims that Leonardo da Vinci was a Grand Master of the Priory of Sion, the ancient society that kept the secret of Jesus and Mary Magdalene, and that he left clues in his paintings concerning his belief in the sacred feminine and the marriage of Jesus and Mary Magdalene. Most significantly, the book claims that in his painting of the Last Supper, Leonardo placed Mary in the honored position at Jesus' right hand, filling the painting with symbols revealing Mary's status as the "Holy Grail" and epitome of the sacred feminine.

The Da Vinci Code claims:

"Sophie examined the figure to Jesus' immediate right [in Leonardo's Last Supper]...It was without a doubt...female.... 'Who is she?' Sophie asked. 'That, my dear,' Teabing replied, 'is Mary Magdalene.'" (*DVC,* p. 243 [263])

"*The Last Supper* practically shouts at the viewer that Jesus and Mary were a pair." (*DVC,* p. 244 [264]; spoken by Teabing)

"Even before Teabing traced the contour for her, Sophie saw it – the indisputable V shape at the focal point of the painting. It was the same symbol Langdon had drawn earlier for the Grail, the chalice, and the female womb." (*DVC,* p. 244 [264])

Does Mary Magdalene appear in Leonardo da Vinci's painting of the Last Supper?

Art historians say no. The figure at Jesus' right has always been recognized as the apostle John, not Mary Magdalene. There is overwhelming evidence that this is so:

(1) John is not seen elsewhere in the painting. This would be a shocking omission since John was present at the meal, and since the Fourth Gospel says he was sitting next to Jesus (John 13:23). If the person to the right of Jesus were a woman, then we must ask, "Where is John?"

(2) John the apostle is often depicted in Renaissance art as a young, beardless, feminine-looking man. The Last Supper paintings of Domenico Ghirlandaio, Andrea del Castagno and Jacopo (or Giacomo) da Ponte show a similarly soft, young John.[1] This is in line with the tradition that he was the youngest of the disciples. Art historian Elizabeth Levy further explains that John is here portrayed in a classic Renaissance type as the "student": "A favored follower, a protégé, or disciple, is always portrayed as very youthful, long-haired and clean shaven."[2]

(3) In an earlier sketch of the Supper, Leonardo gives indications that this figure is John. He portrays him leaning forward in a pose similar to the posture described for him in John 13:23-25.[3]

(4) Tellingly, nobody in Leonardo's day considered this figure to be a woman, and there is no record of any scandal that such a depiction would surely have provoked. We must therefore conclude that it is only because we are looking at the painting with modern eyes that we see a woman, rather

---

[1] These paintings can be conveniently viewed at http://priory-of-sion.com/dvc/lastsupper.html

[2] Cited by Welborn, *De-coding Da Vinci,* pp. 103-104.

[3] Olson and Miesel, *Da Vinci Hoax,* p. 270.

than the classic Renaissance depiction of a young disciple. Leonardo's own *Saint John the Baptist* depicts John the Baptist similarly as an feminine-looking man with long flowing hair.[4]

(5) Finally, even if Leonardo had painted Mary into the scene, this would still say nothing historically about Jesus and Mary. Leonardo painted *The Last Supper* 1500 years after Jesus lived! There is no historical evidence that Mary Magdalene was actually present at the meal.

Does The Last Supper contain hidden messages related to the sacred feminine?

The Da Vinci Code claims there are many symbols in *The Last Supper* representing the sacred feminine. It is curious that in this same context Langdon notes the phenomenon of *scotoma,* where viewers see what they are expecting to see rather than what is actually there (*DVC,* p. 243 [263]). One wonders whether Dan Brown has his tongue firmly in cheek at this point, since by suggesting certain symbols in the painting he causes the reader to actually see them.

There is certainly all manner of symmetry in *The Last Supper,* as in most great art. So it is not surprising that "V"s (supposedly representing the sacred feminine) and "M"s (supposedly standing for *Matrimonio* or *Mary Magdalene*) can be found by looking for them. It seems to me the "M" is more like a "W" with two symmetrical "V"s on either side of Jesus – framing him in the center of the painting. The simple point is that countless shapes and letters could be discerned by the patterns and symmetries, and almost any "code" at all could be proposed from these.

Other claims related to the painting are equally dubious. We discussed the absence of a chalice or grail in the last chapter (pp. 83-84). Two responses may be made to this.

---

[4] Olson and Miesel, *Da Vinci Hoax,* pp. 269-70.

First, as we have said, the idea of a large bejeweled chalice comes from later Grail legends. The Gospels mention only a "cup," which *does* appear in Leonardo's painting. Second, and more importantly, the painting is not meant to depict the institution of the Eucharist but rather the scene in John's Gospel where Jesus predicts his betrayal.[5] The text reads:

> After he had said this, Jesus was troubled in spirit and testified, "Very truly I tell you, one of you is going to betray me." His disciples stared at one another, at a loss to know which of them he meant. One of them, the disciple whom Jesus loved [John], was reclining next to him. Simon Peter motioned to this disciple and said, "Ask him which one he means." (John 13:21-24)

Leonardo's painting captures this moment.[6] The cup is not prominent because the painting is about the response of the disciples to Jesus' prediction. This also explains the actions of Peter in the painting. *The Da Vinci Code* claims Peter is threatening "Mary" by motioning with his hand across her throat. But the text in John's Gospel confirms that Peter, with a look of dismay at Jesus' depressing words, is leaning toward John to say, "Ask him which one he means" (John 13:24). *The Da Vinci Code* also notes a strange "disembodied" hand holding a dagger, presumably meant to threaten "Mary." In fact, the hand is Peter's, and the sword is the one that he will shortly wield in the Garden of Gethsemane (John 18:10-11). If Leonardo wanted to portray Peter as threatening "Mary," he surely would have placed the sword in Peter's left hand, near her throat!

---

[5] John's Gospel does not describe the institution of the Lord's Supper, perhaps another reason why Leonardo did not place a prominent chalice on the table.

[6] Serge Bramly, *Leonardo: Discovering the Life of Leonardo da Vinci* (tr. Siân Reynolds; New York: HarpereCollins, 1991), p. 277.

Is Leonardo's Mona Lisa an androgynous self-portrait representing the sacred feminine?

The Da Vinci Code claims that Leonardo da Vinci intentionally painted the Mona Lisa as an androgynous figure (both male and female) and that he named it "Mona Lisa" as an anagram for the Egyptian god *Amon* and the goddess *Isis* – thus paying homage to the sacred feminine (*DVC,* pp. 120-121 [129-30]).

This claim represents still another flight of fancy. It is true that the woman in the painting remains a mystery, and many theories have been proposed for her identity.[7] The one suggested in *The Da Vinci Code* – that Leonardo used himself as the model – is considered "the most farfetched theory" by art historians.[8] Most consider her to be Mona Lisa Gherardini, the wife of Francesco del Giocondo. In Italy the painting is known as *La Gioconda.*

The suggestion that Leonardo named the *Mona Lisa* after the god Amon and the goddess Isis is simply false. Leonardo did not even name the painting, and the earliest royal inventories call it either "a courtesan in gauze veil" or "a virtuous Italian lady."[9] It wasn't until 1550, thirty years after Leonardo's death, that Giorgio Vasari, in his famous work *The Lives of the Artists,* referred to the painting's subject as "Monna Lisa," the wife of Francesco del Giocondo.[10] *Monna*

---

[7] Bramly, *Leonardo,* p. 362, notes that there about a dozen possible identifications of the sitter.

[8] Bramly, *Leonardo,* p. 363. Alessandro Vezzosi, *Leonardo Da Vinci: The Mind of the Renaissance* (New York: Harry N. Abrams, 1997), p. 125, calls the theory "absurd."

[9] Bramly, *Leonardo,* p. 363. See also Pietro C. Marani, *Leonardo da Vinci: The Complete Paintings* (New York: Harry N. Abrams, Inc., 2003), p. 183 and D. M. Field, *Leonardo Da Vinci* (Regency House, 2002).

[10] Giorgio Vasari, *Lives of the Most Eminent Painters, Sculptors, and Architects* (abridged from the translation by Gaston DuC. DeVere; New York: Random

(shortened to "Mona" in English) is a contraction of *madonna,* meaning *madame*, so the name means "Madame Lisa."

House, 1959), p. 203. The text can be accessed at www.artist-biography.info/artist/leonardo_da_vinci/

CHAPTER 8

THE PRIORY OF SION & THE KNIGHTS TEMPLAR

The Da Vinci Code claims that the Priory of Sion was a secret society formed in 1099 by King Godfrey de Bouillon, shortly after he conquered the city of Jerusalem during the Crusades. Godfrey supposedly formed the society to keep a secret passed down in his family from the time of Christ: Jesus' marriage to Mary Magdalene. The Priory of Sion in turn created a military arm, the Knights Templar, which was given the task of uncovering documents purportedly hidden beneath the Jerusalem temple, documents that would confirm the ancient secret. The Knights discovered these "*Sangreal* documents" and subsequently became fabulously wealthy, either through blackmail or because the Church bought their silence. By the 1300s, their power and influence had become a major threat to the Vatican, which launched a campaign of terror, labeling the Knights Templar heretics and evildoers. The Knights' ranks were decimated, but their secret documents were never discovered, kept hidden by the elusive members of the Priory of Sion.

Though a tantalizing story, this yarn has barely a hint of truth. As we shall see, the Priory of Sion did not even exist until the 1950s. Its pseudo-history was a giant hoax propagated by the Frenchman Pierre Plantard (1920-2000), a con artist with a previous conviction for fraud who was trying to prove he was the legitimate heir to the French throne. The Knights Templar became wealthy through banking, not blackmail, and their destruction by King Philip IV was based on greed and a struggle for power rather than on secrets related to Jesus and Mary Magdalene.

The Da Vinci Code claims:

"FACT: The Priory of Sion – a European secret society founded in 1099– is a real organization. In 1975 Paris's Bibliothèque Nationale discovered parchments known as *Les Dossiers Secrets,* identifying numerous members of the Priory of Sion, including Sir Isaac Newton, Botticelli, Victor Hugo, and Leonardo da Vinci." (*DVC,* p. 1)

"During their years in Jerusalem, the Priory learned of a stash of hidden documents buried beneath the ruins of Herod's temple… These documents, they believed, corroborated Godefroi's powerful secret and were so explosive in nature that the Church would stop at nothing to get them." (*DVC,* p. 158 [171]; spoken by Langdon)

"In order to retrieve the documents from within the ruins, the Priory created a military arm – a group of nine knights called the Order of the Poor Knights of Christ and the Temple of Solomon…More commonly known as the Knights Templar." (*DVC,* p. 158 [171]; spoken by Langdon)

What is the Priory of Sion?

Was the Priory of Sion an ancient society that guarded the secrets of Jesus and Mary Magdalene? Although there was a crusader-era monastic order known as the *Ordre de Notre Dame de Sion* ("Order of Our Lady of Zion"), this group has no relationship to the modern-day Priory of Sion, which was created by Pierre Plantard and some associates, and subsequently used by him to propagate a legend intended to promote his own political agenda.[1]

[1] Primary source research related to the Priory of Sion may be found at Paul Smith's website, priory-of-sion.com. Smith has spent twenty years investigating

The real Priory of Sion

The modern Priory of Sion was founded in 1956 in the French town of Annemasse. French law requires all organizations to be registered with the government and the Priory's official registration is dated July 20, 1956. Its founders were Pierre Plantard, Andrè Bonhomme, and two others. The society was named after a hill south of Annemasse, known as *Mont Sion,* French for "Mount Zion." This name would prove significant in Plantard's later use of the society, since the original Mount Zion is the hill on the southeastern side of Jerusalem, known also as the city of David (see 2 Sam. 5:7).[2] The purpose for Plantard's society, as stated in its founding articles, was "education and mutual aid of the members." A journal known as *Circuit,* an acronym for the French "Chivalry of Catholic Rule and Institution of Independent Traditionalist Union," was published by the society. The contents of the journal suggest that the society was functioning as a local political organization, promoting

---

the hoax. See also Massimo Introvigne's articles "Beyond The Da Vinci Code: History and Myth of the Priory of Sion" available at www.cesnur.org/2005/pa_introvigne.htm and "The Da Vinci Code FAQ," at www.cesnur.org/2005/mi_02_03d.htm; Robert Richardson, "The Priory of Sion Hoax," Gnosis, no. 51 (Spring, 1999), 49-55; available at www.alpheus.org/html/articles/esoteric_history/richardson1.html. For good summaries of the evidence see Olson and Miesel, *The Da Vinci Hoax,* 223-239; Richard Abanes, *The Truth Behind the Da Vinci Code* (Eugene, OR: Harvest House, 2004), pp. 48-57; and at the wikipedia.org article on the Priory of Sion. Various books debunking the myth are in Italian, French and Portuguese and have not yet been translated into English: Massimo Introvigne, *Gli Illuminati e il Priorato di Sion* (Piemme, Milano 2005); Jean-Jacques Bedu, *Les sources secrètes du Da Vinci Code* (Éditions du Rocher, 2005); Marie-France Etchegoin and Frédéric Lenoir, *Code Da Vince: L'Enquête* (Éditions Robert Laffont, Paris, 2004), Bernardo Sanchez Da Motta, *Do Enigma de Rennes-le-Château ao Priorado de Siao - Historia de um Mito Moderno* (Esquilo, 2005).

[2] In the Old Testament "Zion" is used in poetic contexts as another name for Jerusalem (see for example Ps. 102:21).

low-cost housing, providing bus service, and influencing local elections.[3]

To comprehend Plantard's motivations, one must understand French politics of his day. Plantard was anti-Semitic and anti-Masonic, an advocate for the restoration of the French monarchy. The Freemasons had been a powerful force in French politics for many years, and conspiracy buffs claimed they were controlled by powerful Jewish interests. Royalists, composed of supporters of the old royalty system, the Catholic church and far-right political parties stood in opposition to Freemasons, secularists and other advocates of democratically elected governments.[4] The Priory was therefore founded to promote the royalist and Catholic cause.

Bérenger Saunière and the treasure of Rennes-le-Château

Although the original Priory of Sion ceased activities after about a year, Plantard used the society's name for a number of fraudulent activities in the decades that followed. He had come across a legend concerning Bérenger Saunière (1852-1917), a local parish priest in the French village of Rennes-le-Château. (Dan Brown names the murdered curator of the Louvre Jacques Saunière, evidently in honor of the Saunière legend.) According to the legend, Saunière had discovered a hidden treasure in the parish church, a treasure that made him fabulously wealthy. Scholars have since debunked this legend. Saunière never became a millionaire, and no evidence exists that he discovered any treasure. Saunière *did* become financially secure, but it was not through any treasure but through "trafficking in masses," that is, fraudulently charging for the celebration of thousands of masses. The legend of the treasure was apparently created by Noël Corbu (1912-1968),

[3] "Priory of Sion," wikipedia article, pars. 1-4; Introvigne, "Beyond *The Da Vinci Code*," par. 10.
[4] Richardson, "Priory of Sion Hoax," par. 3.

a restaurant owner and one-time detective fiction writer who had purchased Saunière's properties in 1953. Corbu is said to have created the story to bring tourists to the property.[5]

Les Dossiers secrets and the Priory's Grand Masters

Plantard learned of the Saunière legend through his friendship with Corbu and subsequently embellished it for his own purposes. The "treasure" became not gold or jewels but secret documents. Together with his friend, Philippe de Chérisey, Plantard composed these documents in the 1960s and planted them in the Bibliothèque Nationale in Paris and other libraries throughout France. The documents – which were subsequently "discovered" – claimed that the Merovingian line of kings, which ruled in what is now France from the late fifth century to about AD 750,[6] were the legitimate heirs to the French throne and that Plantard himself was in this line.[7] The documents also claimed that the secret society known as the Prieuré de Sion (Priory of Sion), had been formed in AD 1099. Through his research, Plantard had discovered the monastic Order of Our Lady of Zion, founded in Jerusalem in 1099 by Godfrey de Bouillon. Although this abbey had nothing to do with Plantard's own Priory of Sion, the coincidence of names enabled him to claim ancient roots

---

[5] Introvigne, "Beyond *The Da Vinci Code*," par. 13; cf. Paul Smith, "Rennes-le-Château and the Bérenger Saunière Affair Chronology," http://priory-of-sion.com/psp/id91.html; *idem*, "Rennes-le-Château Debunked," http://priory-of-sion.com/psp/id91.html. Other books debunking the Saunière legend include *The Treasure of Rennes-le-Château - A Mystery Solved* (2005) by Bill Putnam and John Edwin Wood; *Mythologie du trésor de Rennes* (1974) by René Descadeillas, and *Autopsie d'un mythe* (1990) by Jean-Jacques Bedu. See also the works cited in note 1 above.

[6] The Merovingian king Clovis I conquered Gaul during his reign, which ran from AD 481-511. Merovingian rule ended in AD 751, when the Carolingian Pepin the Short (the father of Charlemagne) had himself proclaimed king.

[7] Introvigne, "Da Vinci Code FAQ," pars. 2-3.

for his secret society.[8] One of Plantard's forged documents, *Les Dossiers secrets de Henri Lobineau* (called in *The Da Vinci Code* simply *Les Dossiers secrets*) contained a list of the Grand Masters of the Priory of Sion, including Sir Isaac Newton, Victor Hugo, Leonardo da Vinci, and many others.[9] Plantard's documents were published by a friend, Gérard de Sède, in his 1967 book *L'Or de Rennes*. It should be noted that these secret papers said nothing about Jesus and Mary Magdalene nor about any royal bloodline. This twist in the story would come later.

All three of the key perpetuators of this fraud – Philippe de Chérisey, who helped forge the documents, Gérard de Sède, who first published them, and Pierre Plantard himself – later admitted through interviews and in writing that the whole thing was a fake.[10] Yet by this time the fantastic tale had been picked up by others and achieved a life of its own.

The legend grows: Holy Blood, Holy Grail

The expansion of the story – and the version developed in *The Da Vinci Code* – came about primarily through the work of Henry Lincoln, Michael Baigent and Richard Leigh. Henry Lincoln, an English scriptwriter and actor whose real name was Henry Soskin, came into contact with Plantard in the 1970s.[11] He convinced the BBC to produce three documentaries on the Priory, which aired between 1972 and

---

[8] The Order of Our Lady of Mt. Zion ceased to exist in 1617, when it was absorbed by the Jesuit order (Richardson, "Priory of Zion Hoax," par. 17).

[9] Abanes, *Da Vinci Code,* p. 52, citing Paul Smith's online resources (priory-of-sion.com).

[10] For evidence of these admissions see, Introvigne, "Beyond *The Da Vinci Code,*" p. 18; *idem,* "Da Vinci Code FAQ," par. 3. Plantard acknowledged in an interview that *Les Dossier secrets* had been forged (Noël Pinot, "L'Interview de Mr. Pierre Plantard de Saint-Clair," *Vaincre* [2a series], n. 1, April 1989); cited by Introvigne, "Da Vinci Code FAQ," par. 3.

[11] See Paul Smith, "Henry Lincoln (real name, Henry Soskin)," at http://priory-of-sion.com/posd/soskin.html.

1979. Lincoln then collaborated with Michael Baigent and Richard Leigh to write their 1982 book, *Holy Blood, Holy Grail.* The book merged Plantard's theories with many others, especially those of Robert Ambelain (1907-1997), who in 1970 had published a book called *Jésus ou le mortel secret des templiers,* which claimed that Jesus had a partner or concubine named Salome.[12] *Holy Blood, Holy Grail* changed Salome to Mary Magdalene and blended the story with legends related to the Knights Templar, the Freemasons and the Holy Grail. Jesus was married to Mary Magdalene and intended her to lead his church. After Jesus' crucifixion, she fled with her child to southern Gaul with Joseph of Arimathea. Her descendants married into the Merovingian dynasty of French kings in the fifth century. In 1099, the Merovingian king and crusader Godfrey of Bouillon conquered Jerusalem and founded the Priory of Sion, which, in turn, created the Knights Templar. The Knights retrieved secret documents related to Mary Magdalene and Jesus that were buried in the ruins of the Jerusalem Temple.

It is this bizarre and unverifiable version of events that Dan Brown borrowed *en masse* in *The Da Vinci Code.* Brown conveniently ignores the many books and articles, as well as a BBC documentary in 1996, that debunked the origins of the Priory of Sion.[13] Indeed, in their 1986 book *The Messianic Legacy,* Lincoln, Baigent and Leigh acknowledge that Plantard was a con man and that many of his documents were fake, but they continue to claim that other evidence related to the Priory of Sion and Jesus' descendants is true.[14]

---

[12] Introvigne, "Da Vinci Code FAQ," par. 5.

[13] "Timewatch: The History of a Mystery," BBC 2 (InVision Productions), aired 17 September 1996. See Paul Smith, http://priory-of-sion.com/dvc/documentaries.html for other documentaries related to the Priory of Sion and Rennes-le-Château.

[14] Introvigne, "Da Vinci Code FAQ," par. 6.

Plantard changes his story

Plantard himself sought a comeback in 1989 with a new version of his story. He rejected the documents he had "discovered" in the 1960s and created new lists of Grand Masters for the Priory of Sion. He now claimed that the Priory did not go back to Godfrey of Bouillon and the Knights Templar, but only to 1681 and was linked with St. Vincent de Paul. His new legend had nothing to do with Jesus Christ or the Merovingian dynasty, but rather claimed extraordinary transformational power that came from certain black rocks of a mountain near Rennes-le-Château. Coincidentally, Plantard himself had recently purchased this property.[15]

This new myth, however, was Plantard's undoing. The man he identified as his immediate predecessor as Grand Master of the Priory of Sion, Roger-Patrice Pelat, was a prominent public figure and a close friend of French President François Mitterand. Pelat became involved in a securities scandal and subsequently committed suicide. During the investigation, police searched Plantard's house and discovered many forged Priory documents, some claiming he was the true king of France. Plantard confessed under oath that the whole business was a fabrication. He lived in obscurity until his death on February 3, 2000.[16] Unfortunately for the truth, his fanciful story continues to live on in books like *Holy Blood, Holy Grail* and *The Da Vinci Code.*

---

[15] Introvigne, "Beyond *The Da Vinci Code,*" par. 19; Olson and Miesel, *The Da Vinci Hoax,* p. 238.

[16] Olson and Miesel, *The Da Vinci Hoax,* p. 238; Abanes, *Da Vinci Code,* p. 54, citing Paul Smith's online articles (priory-of-sion.com).

Who were the Knights Templar?

Were the Knights Templar the military wing of the Priory of Sion that discovered secret documents about Jesus and Mary Magdalene under the Jerusalem Temple? Since the Priory of Sion never existed in the form *The Da Vinci Code* asserts, the Knights Templar could hardly have been their military wing. There are innumerable legends concerning the Knights, arising especially because of their great wealth and because of their violent destruction at the hands of King Philip IV of France. The truth in fact is very different from that described in *The Da Vinci Code.*

The Real Knights Templar[17]

The Knights Templar were a monastic order of knights established by Hugh des Payens and eight companions in 1118 after the conquest of Jerusalem during the Crusades. Known also as the Order of the Poor Knights of Christ and of the Temple of Solomon, their purpose was to protect the holy sites and the pilgrims visiting them. The Knights gained credibility when they were supported by the influential Bernard of Clairvaux. Bernard wrote the Templars' rule, basing it on his own Cistercian Order. A papal bull of AD 1139 made the Knights independent of local bishops and answerable only to the papacy. Similar independence from local authority had been granted to other military orders, like the Knights Hospitaller, their chief rivals in the Holy Land. The Templars, like other monastic orders of knights, were

[17] For primary source material related to the Templars, see Malcolm Barber and Keith Bate, *The Templars. Selected sources translated and annotated* (Manchester and New York: Manchester University Press, 2002). For factual histories see Malcolm Barber, *The New Knighthood: A History of the Order of the Temple* (New York: Cambridge University Press, 1994); Stephen Howarth, *The Knights Templar* (New York: Macmillan, 1982); Edward Burman, *The Templars: Knights of God* (Rochester, Vermont: Destiny Books, 1986); G. Grosschmid, "Templars," *New Catholic Encyclopedia* (Palatine, IL: Jack Heraty & Associates, 1967), vol. XIII, pp. 992-994.

immensely popular during the early Crusades, receiving large gifts and stipends from kings and wealthy patrons. They also became famous for their rigorous discipline and military prowess, and they were involved in every major battle in the Holy Land during the Crusades.

The Templars' influence in the Holy Land diminished as Muslim armies gradually re-conquered the holy sites. At the same time, their influence in Europe continued to rise. According to *The Da Vinci Code,* this wealth and power came from blackmailing the church or because the Vatican bought their silence concerning the "truth" about Jesus and Mary Magdalene. In reality, the Templars accumulated their wealth and landholdings through large donations and by developing an international banking system, becoming lenders to the rich and powerful throughout Europe.

It was the Templars' wealth and power that eventually resulted in their fall. *The Da Vinci Code* claims that Pope Clement V secretly launched a plot against them, arresting, torturing and murdering them throughout Europe (*DVC,* pp. 159-160 [173]). In fact, it was King Philip IV ("the Fair") of France – strapped for cash and envious for the Templars' wealth – who instigated the persecution. He ordered all Templars in France (not throughout all Europe as *The Da Vinci Code* claims) to be arrested. In a series of raids on Friday, October 13, 1307, the Knights were rounded up and accused of all manner of heresies and abominations. Many were tortured and burned at the stake. Others fled the country.

Although Pope Clement V had little to do with Philip's original plot, the papacy was very weak at this time and functioned at the whim of the French court. Under pressure from Philip, the Pope ordered the Templars to be put on trial throughout Europe. *The Da Vinci Code* fails to mention that in Germany, Spain, Portugal, Italy and England, the Templars were found mostly innocent. Yet the damage had been done and the order was officially dissolved by the Council of Vienne in 1312. Their property was given to the order of the Hospitallers. The last Grand Master of the Templars, Jacques de Molay, was burned at the stake in 1314.[18]

Legends about the Templars

Though the devastation wreaked by King Philip marked the historical end of the Templars, it was only the beginning of the many legends and myths created about them.[19] Their wealth and power, together with the treachery and violence associated with their destruction, proved fertile ground for the imagination of conspiracy theorists. While it is well beyond our scope to deal with the origin and history of these myths, the Templars have been linked to almost every secret society, esoteric religion, or conspiracy myth associated with the Middle Ages. Their activities have been said to include witchcraft, idolatry, goddess worship and Gnostic rituals. Among their secret possessions have been claimed Christ's crown of thorns, the Ark of the Covenant, the Shroud of Turin, and – of course – the Holy Grail.

It certainly did not slow the growth of these legends that the equally mysterious society of Freemasons came to be associated with the Knights Templar. This connection appears to have been made first by Chevalier Ramsay, who claimed in a speech given in 1736 that the ancestors of the Freemasons were crusaders who had access to ancient wisdom. This wisdom was partly biblical, derived from the Old Testament patriarchs and the builders of the temple, but "also reflected Egyptian and Greek mysteries, and other hidden secrets of the

---

[18] On the trials of the Templars, see Malcolm Barber, *The Trial of the Templars* (Cambridge, Eng.; New York: Cambridge University Press, 1978). For good summaries, see Grosschmid, "Templars," 993-94; P. Schaff, *History of the Christian Church* (Grand Rapids: Eerdmans, 1949-1952), vol. VI, pp. 52-54.

[19] See especially Peter Partner, *The Murdered Magicians: The Templars and Their Myth* (Oxford: University Press: 1982).

pagan world."[20] Though Ramsay did not directly link the Knights Templar to the Freemasons, many others after him did:

> Once the myth-making process had begun, and the Crusaders had been pushed to the forefront of supposed Masonic history, the temptation to 'speculative' Masons to draw the Templars into their symbolic system was great. The temple is the centre of the whole architectural metaphor on which Freemasonry is built.[21]

In addition to the Freemasons, many unaffiliated esoteric and occultic groups today claim the name and heritage of the Knights Templar.

The dubious connection of the Knights to the Holy Grail was developed by Josef von Hammer-Purgstall in his 1818 book *Mystery of Baphomet Revealed.* Hammer-Purgstall claimed the Templars revered an androgynous idol named Baphomet, also known as Sophia, which they worshipped with ritual orgies.[22] They were also said to be guardians of the Holy Grail, which was not the cup of the Last Supper, but some kind of Gnostic knowledge. Recent works like *The Templar Revelation* and *Holy Blood, Holy Grail* draw heavily on Hammer-Purgstall's theories connecting the Templars to paganism, witchcraft and Mother-Goddess worship.[23]

The Da Vinci Code borrows its Templar myths primarily from *Holy Blood, Holy Grail* and *The Templar Revelation.* Corrections concerning the Templars include the following:

---

[20] Partner, *Murdered Magicians,* pp. 103-104.
[21] Partner, *Murdered Magicians,* p. 105.
[22] Partner, *Murdered Magicians,* 109, 138-145. Baphomet was originally an old French name for the prophet Mohammed.
[23] Olson and Miesel, *The Da Vinci Hoax,* 216-217.

(1) As noted above, the Knights Templar were not founded by the Priory of Sion, but by Hugh de Payens and eight of his fellow knights. Their task was to protect the Holy Land and its Christian pilgrims.

(2) The Templars achieved their wealth through wealthy patrons and through their skills as financial managers, not through blackmail or extortion.

(3) There is no evidence that the Templars excavated below the Jerusalem Temple or that they discovered any treasure, whether the Ark of the Covenant, the Shroud of Turin, the Holy Grail, or secret documents concerning Jesus. Langdon's claim in *The Da Vinci Code* that "all academics agree" that the Knights discovered "something that made them wealthy and powerful beyond anyone's wildest imagination" (*DVC,* p. 158 [172]) is simply false.

(4) Though the Templars were certainly secretive, there is no credible evidence that they practiced pagan worship, witchcraft, Gnostic rituals or goddess worship. Confessions of idolatry by some Templars during their trials were gained under the duress of torture, hardly admissible (or reliable) evidence in a legitimate court. Their greatest sins appear to have been avarice and pride.

(5) It was King Philip IV, not Pope Clement V, who instigated the persecution against the Templars, and the motivation was jealousy and greed rather than any attempt to protect supposed secrets of the Grail.

(6) Most of the claims about the Templars concerning architecture and art made in *The Da Vinci Code* also have little basis in fact. The Templars did not create Gothic architecture, nor does the round style of some Templar churches indicate a pagan influence (*DVC,* p. 339 [366]). Many Templar churches were not round and there are non-

Templar churches that are round – most notably the Church of the Holy Sepulchre in Jerusalem.[24]

[24] See details in Olson and Miesel, *The Da Vinci Hoax,* p. 201.

CONCLUSION: SEEKING THE TRUTH

The popularity of *The Da Vinci Code*

What accounts for the amazing success of this book? There are no doubt many factors:

(1) For one thing, it is *a great story.* While few would call *The Da Vinci Code* great literature, it is certainly *great entertainment,* a gripping suspense novel that leaves you hanging at the end of each chapter and wanting more. Just ask anyone who has stayed up until the early hours of the morning because they just couldn't put it down. It is a great story.

But believers in the real Jesus Christ have a *better story.* In fact, it is *the greatest story ever told.* The overarching drama (the "meta-narrative") of the Bible tells us who we are in relation to God and in relationship with one another. It tells us that God created us in his image to be in communion with him. In contrast to the Gnostic worldview, this physical world was created "very good" as a thing of great beauty and value, worth cherishing and protecting. While Gnosticism claimed the distinction between male and female resulted from a fracturing of our true spiritual identity, the Bible celebrates sexual diversity as part of God's good creation. Man and woman together form complete humanity, perfect complements and equally valuable in God's eyes.

The Bible also tells us, however, that something has gone terribly wrong with this perfect world and with the human condition. The great story took a tragic turn when Adam and Eve rebelled against God and turned their backs on him. The world entered a fallen state. Disease, death, personal tragedy, relational conflict and even natural disasters are all a result of the fallen and decaying state of creation. Yet as in any great story, this conflict gave way to hope and resolution. At the climax of the meta-narrative God himself entered human history in the person of Jesus Christ. He became one of us, real flesh and blood humanity. As the hero of the story, he set aside his own ambition and power and gave himself wholly for others. He suffered and died so that others could live. The result was the creation of a new humanity with a restored relationship with their Creator. While *The Da Vinci Code* is a great yarn, it pales in comparison to the greatest story ever told.

(2) Another reason for *The Da Vinci Code's* great success is because it taps well into our culture of anti-authoritarianism, personal fulfillment, and post-Christian spirituality. The real Jesus called on people to set aside their own selfish desires and to live in submission to God and in self-sacrificial love for others. He said true believers must take up their cross and follow him, dying to self. The model for this was Jesus himself, who paid the penalty for our sins through his death on the cross. Jesus was completely focused on others rather than himself. In the Garden of Gethsemane he agonized over his coming fate, desiring to escape the pain of the cross. Yet he willingly submitted to the Father's purpose, saying "not as I will, but as you will."[1] The Bible teaches that salvation comes through admitting our sinfulness and trusting wholly in God for our salvation, living in dependence on him through faith. It means faith in Christ's work on the cross rather than our own good deeds.

Gnosticism, by contrast, claimed that salvation came from within, a recognition of one's true spiritual identity. It was not submission to some external authority, but freedom through self-enlightenment. There are striking parallels between ancient Gnosticism and today's New Age movement. For both, humanity's problem is not sin and rebellion against God, but ignorance, a failure to recognize the god and the

---

[1] Matt. 26:39; Mark 8:34; Luke 22:42.

good within. Salvation comes not through faith in God, but through finding the light within oneself.

This striking contrast places the worldview of Gnosticism on a collision course with that of Christianity. Either Jesus was a self-enlightened mystic, teaching people to find salvation within themselves, or he was Israel's Messiah, the promised Savior who called on people to repent and submit to God's kingdom and authority. Either Jesus taught people the secret mysteries of self-discovery, or he willingly went to the cross to pay the penalty for their sins. The latter perspective is not very popular in our culture today. People don't want to be told that they must submit to an authority outside of themselves. They don't want to be told that the greatest good is living for others instead of for themselves. They want freedom to pursue personal happiness and self-fulfillment.

Yet the message of Christianity is that our salvation was accomplished not through an act of power or self-fulfillment, but through Christ's sacrificial death for others. We will only find true fulfillment and our true purpose in life when we do the same, living not for ourselves but for God and for others.

(3) A third reason for *The Da Vinci Code's* success is because it is delightfully scandalous. People love a good scandal, especially when it means the fall of the high and mighty. In this case the arrogant villain is the Roman Catholic Church, which supposedly has suppressed the truth and squashed all opposition for two thousand years. Yet as we have seen, the real scandal of *The Da Vinci Code* is that people are swallowing hook, line and sinker these ridiculous claims, simply because they are packaged in an entertaining and scholarly-sounding manner.

Even here, however, Christians have a better "scandal" than *The Da Vinci Code.* The New Testament calls it the scandal of the cross. It is the shocking reality that one of the most hideous forms of execution ever devised – crucifixion –

in fact became the means of salvation for the whole world. The apostle Paul says that the cross of Christ is a "stumbling block to Jews" and "foolishness to Greeks," but to those who have been transformed by its message, it is "the power of God and the wisdom of God" (1 Cor. 1:22-25). The cross reminds us that, despite the injustice and suffering in this world, and despite the apparent triumph of evil, God can take that evil and turn it into good. He can use the horrific injustice done to his own Son and bring from it salvation and redemption to a fallen world. That is a scandal worth passing on to others.

(4) Another reason for *The Da Vinci Code's* appeal is because it purports to be pro-women and pro-liberation. Christianity is presented as a male-dominated and oppressive institution that has enslaved and subjugated women throughout history. Yet *The Da Vinci Code's* "liberation" is comprised mainly of ritualistic sex acts performed publicly in front of crowds of "fellow-worshippers." Most women I know would not view this as very liberating, but more like an adolescent male fantasy. It seems to me true Christianity's view of women and sex is far more liberating than that of *The Da Vinci Code*. The Bible calls women and men to live in lifelong, loving, mutually-affirming and sexually-fulfilling monogamous relationships, where each partner seeks to bring out the best in the other and to enable them to be all that God calls them to be.

It is certainly true that fallen human nature often results in abuse, oppression and the exploitation of women (and men). Dysfunctional families, abusive relationships, and sexist attitudes are rampant throughout our society and throughout the world. But such behaviors are totally contrary to Jesus' teaching and to what God calls his people to be. Indeed, while the church has not been immune to sexism and misogyny, historically Christians have been agents of liberation for women. It was the early Christians who often rescued baby girls who were "exposed" – abandoned and left to die – in the Greco-Roman world. It was Christian missionaries in India who opposed the practice of Sati, the burning of a widow upon her husband's funeral pyre, as well as the modern practice of bride-burning. Christian organizations have led the way in providing food relief and health services to women and children in famine-ravaged and war-torn countries. It is Christians who have sought to rescue women from slave prostitution and from exploitation as child brides in developing countries. And Christians have pushed hard for equal rights and protections for women under oppressive Muslim regimes. While the church's historical record regarding women has certainly not been spotless, *The Da Vinci Code* fails to acknowledge that it is Christianity, not paganism, which has led the way in promoting the rights of women around the world.

(5) A final reason I think *The Da Vinci Code* is so popular is because it gives an ancient story contemporary relevance. How exciting to think that Jesus' descendants could be among us today. This is better than an Elvis sighting!

But of course Christians know that it is not just Jesus' descendants, but Jesus himself who is present in the world today. Jesus told his disciples that, although he was leaving, he would be with them through his Spirit. He is now present through his "body" – the church – made up of all true believers. We are his hands and his feet. We show *his compassion* by reaching out to the poor and the weak. We demonstrate *his love* by loving others – even our enemies. We reveal *his justice* by speaking out against injustice. We exhibit *his passion for truth* by speaking out against falsehood and lies.

Why are Christians so bothered by the book? For one thing, it is not true. But what is worse, its inaccuracies concern what Christians view as the most important thing in life: the abundant life and eternal salvation available through Jesus Christ. The bottom line with reference to Christianity and *The Da Vinci Code,* then, is "Who was Jesus Christ?" Was he merely a human teacher who was later deified by his enthusiastic followers, or was he the divine Son of God who brought redemption to a lost and dying world?

Who did Jesus claim to be?

We have already seen that Christians in the first century were already worshipping Jesus as the divine Son of God and the Savior of the world (see Chapter 1, pp. 20-23). *But were these beliefs misguided?* What did Jesus really claim about himself? Jesus' most explicit claims appear in the Fourth Gospel, the Gospel of John. There Jesus says that whoever has seen him, has seen God the Father (14:9). He claims to be the "I AM" who existed before Abraham, a title recalling God's self identification in Exodus 3:14.[2] Jesus shares God's attributes: he is the giver and sustainer of life;[3] he will raise the dead at the final resurrection[4] and will serve as the final judge of all people (John 5:22, 27). He knows all things.[5] As the Son sent from above, he provides the only access to the Father and to eternal life. No one comes to the Father except through him (John 14:6).[6] The Father and the Son operate in complete unity and know one another perfectly.[7]

While these are Jesus' most explicit claims, his words and deed in the other three Gospels – Matthew, Mark and Luke[8] –

---

[2] John 8:24, 28, 58. See page 54 above.
[3] John 5:16-18, 26; 6:27, 35, 50-58.
[4] John 5:21, 25; 4:53; 6:39-40, 44, 54; 10:28; 11:25-26.
[5] John 1:48; 2:24-25; 6:15; 8:14; 13:1, 11; 21:17.
[6] Cf. John 3:16, 36; 4:14; 5:21-26; 6:33, 35, 51-58, 68; 8:12; 10:10, 17-18; 11:25; 17:2-3.
[7] John 10:15, 30; 14:10.
[8] Matthew, Mark and Luke are called the "Synoptic Gospels" because they share many common stories and verbal parallels. The word "synoptic" means "viewed together."

leave no doubt about his divine nature and unique status. Jesus there exercises the attributes of God: he forgives sins,[9] knows people's thoughts[10] and accepts their worship.[11] He will be the judge of all people, determining their eternal destiny.[12] He is the Lord of nature, calming the storm, feeding the multitudes, and walking on water.[13] Following the resurrection he claims to mediate the Holy Spirit – the presence of God – to his people,[14] and promises his divine presence among them.[15]

These are astonishing claims. If true, they would confirm that Jesus is the center-point of human history, the Savior and king whose perfect life and death on the cross brought reconciliation and restoration to a fallen world. But were they true? Or was Jesus a self-deluded prophet or, worse yet, a great deceiver? The ultimate test for the authenticity of Jesus' claims is his own resurrection. If Jesus did not rise from the dead, then his claims to be the Savior of the world were certainly false. If, on the other hand, he did rise, this is proof that God vindicated him as Messiah and Lord (see Acts 2:36).

The evidence for the Resurrection

According to the apostle Paul, Christianity rises or falls on the reality of the resurrection. If Christ rose from the dead, then all that he said was true. If he did not rise, then Christians are affirming and testifying to a lie:

> ...if Christ has not been raised, our preaching is useless and so is your faith. More than that, we are

---

[9] Matt. 9:2; Mark 2:5; Luke 5:20.
[10] Matt. 9:4; Mark 2:8; Luke 5:22; Matt. 12:25.
[11] Matt. 2:11; 14:33; 28:9, 17; Luke 24:52.
[12] Matt. 7:21-23; 25:31-46.
[13] Mark 4:35-41; 6:30-44; 6:47-51 (cf. the parallels in Matthew and Luke).
[14] Luke 24:49; Acts 1:5, 8; 2:33.
[15] Matt. 18:20; 28:20; Acts 16:7.

> then found to be false witnesses about God, for we have testified about God that he raised Christ from the dead.... And if Christ has not been raised, your faith is futile; you are still in your sins. (1 Cor. 15:14-19)

While no historical event can be proven with absolute certainty, certain evidence can be verified beyond reasonable doubt.[16] In the points that follow, I will not assume the absolute reliability of the New Testament, but will take the perspective of a skeptical historian, asking the question, *"What can be known beyond reasonable doubt?"*

(1) The first fact that is beyond reasonable doubt is that Jesus of Nazareth was a real person who died at the hands of Roman authorities in the early first century. No credible scholar today denies Jesus' existence nor the basic fact that he was arrested and crucified in Jerusalem by the Romans around AD 30.

(2) The second near certainty is that Jesus actually died on the cross. Even the most liberal critics scoff at books like *The Passover Plot* by Hugh Schonfield, which claimed Jesus survived the cross and revived in the cool of the tomb. The Romans were experts at crucifixion and could not have botched the job. In any case, a half-dead Jesus emerging from the tomb could scarcely have convinced his disciples he had risen triumphant from the grave.

(3) A third reasonably certain fact is that Joseph of Arimathea, a member of the Jewish Sanhedrin, took the body

---

[16] The most comprehensive volume on the resurrection is the magisterial work of N. T. Wright, *The Resurrection of the Son of God* (Minneapolis: Fortress, 2003). For apologetic defenses of the resurrection, see William Lane Craig, *The Son Rises* (Chicago: Moody, 1981); Gary R. Habermas, *The Resurrection of Jesus* (Grand Rapids: Baker, 1980). For points listed here see chapter 20 of my forthcoming text, *Four Portraits, One Jesus. An Introduction to Jesus and the Gospels* (Grand Rapids: Zondervan).

of Jesus and buried it in his own tomb.[17] There is no reason the church would create such a person or incident unless it actually happened. Joseph's hometown of Arimathea has no symbolic significance that could explain its creation. It is particularly unlikely that the church would create a story where a member of the Sanhedrin – the group that condemned Jesus – performed such an action.

(4) Fourth, the tomb in which Jesus was buried was discovered empty on the third day. Proof of this is, first, that all four Gospels testify that the empty tomb was discovered by *female disciples.* This is remarkable since women were not viewed in first century Judaism as reliable witnesses. If the church had made up these stories, they would never have identified women as the primary witnesses. Second, if the tomb was not empty, the disciples could not have preached the gospel in Jerusalem. But there is indisputable evidence that the church began in Jerusalem shortly after Jesus' death (see Acts 1-2; Gal. 1:18-20). Third, no objection was ever raised to Christianity that the tomb was not empty. In fact, the Jewish claim of a stolen body (Matt. 28:11-15) *presupposes* an empty tomb.

(5) Many credible witnesses saw Jesus alive. While the Gospels record many resurrection appearances, some skeptics claim these are late and legendary accounts. But no one can deny the remarkable evidence presented by the apostle Paul, a contemporary of Jesus who underwent a dramatic conversion to Christianity. In his letter known as First Corinthians (written about AD 55), Paul asserts the reality of the resurrection and claims that more than five hundred people saw Jesus alive – many of whom were still alive (1 Cor. 15:3-8). He essentially challenges his readers to check out the evidence for themselves. Here we have a first person, primary

---

[17] Matt. 27:57; Mark 15:43; Luke 23:51; John 19:38.

source historical account concerning the reality of the resurrection appearances.

(6) Finally, the lives of the disciples were completely transformed. We have to ask what else could account for the transformation of a small band of defeated cowards in a matter of weeks into a group of believers who could not be silenced by any amount of persecution. Something happened on that Sunday morning that changed their lives forever.

Weighing the evidence: the choice is yours

I sometimes hear Christians complain that *The Da Vinci Code* is a disaster for the church. But I don't see it that way. In my opinion, it is not a disaster, but a great opportunity. After all, people who have scarcely thought about Jesus are considering his claims. And I am convinced that anyone who takes the time to honestly examine the evidence will discover *not* the Jesus of *The Da Vinci Code,* but the Jesus of the Gospels, the Messiah who came to earth to offer himself as a sacrifice for sins, to seek and to save the lost (Mark 10:45; Luke 19:10). It is this Jesus who brings hope and purpose to a lost and dying world.

In the end, of course, no amount of historical evidence will convince the confirmed skeptic. But the essence of the gospel is not about historical proofs or arguments for the existence of God. It is about a real relationship with the living God. Two thousand years ago Mary Magdalene and the other women went to the tomb of Jesus, expecting to anoint his dead body. Instead, they discovered an empty tomb and had a real encounter with the living and resurrected Lord. The Bible is an invitation to you to have such encounter with God through his Son Jesus Christ. I hope you will respond to this invitation.

Quick Answer Guide
WITH PAGE REFERENCES

The Identity of Jesus Christ

Did the Council of Nicea turn Jesus into a god?	No. The church had been worshipping Jesus as divine for centuries before Nicea. The NT itself testifies to Jesus' deity (John 1:1). **See pp. 20-21.**
What really happened at Nicea?	The Council rejected the heretical views of Arius and affirmed that Jesus the Son was equal to and co-eternal with God the Father. **See pp. 23-24.**
Did Jesus himself claim to be divine?	Both Jesus' own words and his actions provide very strong evidence for his divine nature. **See pp. 113- 114.**

The Canon of Scripture

Did Constantine support Christianity for political reasons?	Politics always played a role in Constantine's decisions, but the evidence suggests his conversion was authentic. **See p. 26.**
Did Constantine move Christian worship to Sunday in honor of the sun god?	No. Christians were worshiping on Sunday two centuries before Constantine in commemoration of the resurrection of Jesus. **See pp. 26-27.**
Did Christianity adopt pagan symbols?	Sometimes, but they instilled these symbols with Christian meaning, thus transforming their meaning and significance. **See p. 27.**
Did Constantine commission a new Bible?	No. The New Testament books were revered as authoritative Scripture long before Constantine was born. **See pp. 27-31.**

How was the canon of Scripture decided?	Although the church's official acceptance of all 27 books took place gradually, the NT books were being treated as God's inspired Word shortly after they were written. **See pp. 28-31.**
What role did Marcion play in the establishment of the canon?	The heretic Marcion claimed authority for only some NT books. The church rejected Marcion's canon and produced lists of its own. **See pp. 29-30.**
Has the Bible evolved through countless translations?	No. Translations today come from the earliest available ancient manuscripts. **See pp. 31-32.**
Has the Bible been repeatedly revised by the church?	No. The Bible has better manuscript attestation than any other ancient book, confirming that the text we have today is very close to the originals. **See pp. 32-34.**
Did the Bible drop out of the sky from heaven?	No. The Bible claims to be both fully human and fully divine, God's message given through human instruments. **See pp. 34-35.**
How do we know the Bible is God's Word?	The divine authority of the Bible is confirmed through its fulfilled prophecies, its extraordinary unity and coherence, its power to change lives, and the confirmation by the Holy Spirit in the hearts and minds of believers. **See pp. 34-36.**

GNOSTICISM & THE "LOST GOSPELS"

Were the New Testament Gospels chosen over more than eighty others?	No. The NT Gospels were honored by the church as *the authoritative accounts* of Jesus long before the so-called apocryphal gospels were written. **See pp. 38, 39-40, 42-44.**
Were the Gnostic gospels rejected at the Council of Nicea?	No. They were not even discussed. The Gnostic gospels were never seriously considered for inclusion in the canon since they contained doctrines at odds with the teachings of Jesus and the apostles. **See pp. 27-31, 42-47.**

Are the Dead Sea Scrolls "lost gospels"?	No. The Dead Sea Scrolls are a library of books that were collected by the Jewish community at Qumran near the Dead Sea. **See pp. 38-39.**
What are the "lost books" of the New Testament?	The NT Apocrypha is the name given to books written under assumed names (pseudepigraph-ically) after the NT period. **See pp. 39-44.**
What is Gnosticism?	Gnosticism was a second century rival to Christianity which claimed that salvation was achieved through special *gnōsis* ("knowledge") of one's true spiritual identity. **See pp. 40-41.**
What is the Nag Hammadi Library?	A collection of mostly Gnostic writings discovered in 1945 in Egypt. They confirm and expand upon our knowledge of this 2nd century religious movement. **See pp. 42-44.**
Are the Gnostic Gospels the earliest Christian records?	No. The earliest ones likely date to the mid-2nd century. All the NT Gospels can be confidently dated to the 1st century. **See pp. 42-44.**
Do the Gnostic Gospels reveal a merely human Jesus, as DVC *asserts?*	No. The Gnostic books, though diverse, have a strong "docetic" tendency, which means they claim Jesus was a spirit being who only appeared to be human. **See pp. 44-45.**
Do the NT Gospels suppress the humanity of Jesus?	No. The NT Gospels present a much more human Jesus than the later apocryphal or Gnostic Gospels. **See pp. 44-45.**
Was Jesus a Gnostic teacher?	No. Jesus was a 1st century Jew, and the NT Gospels accurately portray him in this Palestinian Jewish context. **See pp. 45-46.**
Was Gnosticism liberating and feminist?	For the most part, no. Although women may have served in some limited leadership roles in Gnosticism, there were also anti-female trends. The Gnostic *Gospel of Thomas* claims that females must become males to enter the kingdom of God (*Thomas,* saying 114). **See pp. 46-47.**

CHRISTIANITY & THE SACRED FEMININE

Did the earliest religion celebrate the "sacred feminine"?	Historians and archaeologists reject this claim. Most pagan religions were animistic or polytheistic, exploiting rather than supporting women. **See pp. pp. 51-53.**
Did the early Jews worship the sacred feminine?	This claim has no historical basis. The Jews were monotheists, worshipping Yahweh, the one true God, who was pure Spirit. **See pp. 53-54.**
Was "Shekinah" Yahweh's female consort?	No. Shekinah is a late rabbinic term for God's glorious presence. It was not a female deity. **See p. 54.**
Is "Jehovah" a merging of names for male and female deities?	No. Jehovah is a mis-pronunciation of Yahweh, God's covenant name revealed to Israel. It has nothing to do with male and female deities. **See pp. 54-55.**
Did the church seek to eradicate the pure religion of the sacred feminine?	There is no reliable evidence for a power struggle between Peter and Mary Magdalene, nor for any suppression of goddess worship during Constantine's time. **See pp. 55-56.**
Did the church burn between five and nine million women as witches?	Though the burning of accused witches was a horrible tragedy, the numbers were closer to forty thousand, and most accusations were not made by church authorities. **See pp. 56-57.**
Were accused witches free-thinking women, priestesses and goddess worshipers?	No. Most accused witches were poor and unpopular women (and men). Also, these witches were seldom (if ever) accused of practicing a pagan or goddess-worshipping religion. **See p. 57.**
Was the early church oppressive to women?	In reality, women were given a higher place in the church than in the rest of Greco-Roman society. Christianity was a great liberating force (see Gal. 3:28). **See pp. 58-59.**

JESUS AND MARY MAGDALENE: HUSBAND AND WIFE?

Was Jesus married?	No. There is no reliable historical evidence that Jesus was married, and much evidence that he was not. **See pp. 62-63.**
Weren't virtually all Jewish men of Jesus' day married?	While most Jewish men of Jesus' day were married, there were many exceptions. **See pp. 62-63.**
Hasn't Jesus' marriage been documented by many historians?	No. There are *no* ancient references to Jesus' marriage. This is a modern idea promoted by tabloid journalists. **See p. 63.**
Don't the Gnostic gospels claim Jesus was married to Mary Magdalene?	No. While the Gnostic gospels describe a special esoteric relationship between Jesus and Mary, it is not a marital or a sexual one. **See pp. 64-69.**
Doesn't Jesus kiss Mary in the Gospel of Philip?	Yes, but it is a kiss of fellowship used to transfer *gnōsis,* or secret "knowledge." Jesus also kisses his other disciples in the same way. **See pp. 66-67.**
Do these Gnostic gospels relate real historical episodes from Jesus' life?	No. Even scholars sympathetic to Gnosticism acknowledge that these are fictional dialogues created by later Gnostics. **See p. 65.**
Aren't Peter and Mary treated as rivals in the Gnostic literature?	Yes, but this is a symbolic representation of the struggle between Christianity and Gnosticism. It has nothing to do with the historical Peter or Mary. **See pp. 67-69.**
If Jesus were married, would this undermine the truth of Christianity?	No. Sexual relations within marriage are part of God's good creation and are celebrated in Scripture. Jesus' sinless nature would not have been damaged by marriage. **See pp. 61, 69-70.**

THE REAL MARY MAGDALENE: FAITHFUL DISCIPLE, PROSTITUTE OR HOLY GRAIL?

Was Mary Magdalene a prostitute?	No, there is no evidence that Mary was a prostitute. This depiction arose from the confusion of several different women in Scripture. **See pp. 72-74.**
What do we know historically about Mary Magdalene?	Mary was healed of demon possession by Jesus; she was one of the women who supported him and his disciples; and she was the first person to see the resurrected Jesus. **See pp. 74-76.**
Did the church demote Mary from her role as Jesus' successor?	There is no evidence for such a demotion. Mary is portrayed positively in the Gospels as the most prominent of the women disciples. The later church honored Mary as a saint. **See pp. 76-80.**
Was Mary from the royal house of Benjamin?	No ancient source identifies Mary's tribal ancestry. Furthermore, there was no royal house of Benjamin with a claim to Israel's throne. **See p. 83.**
Was Mary Magdalene the real "Holy Grail"?	Grail legends did not even arise until the late Middle Ages, over 1000 years after Christ. Even these legends were never connected to Mary or to the sacred feminine. **See pp. 82-84.**
Are the later traditions about Mary Magdalene true?	No. Legends about Mary's journey to France did not appear until the 11th century. We have no reliable historical data beyond the New Testament period. **See pp. 85-87.**
Do these later legends describe Mary's role as Jesus' wife?	No. Even if we were to take these medieval legends seriously, they never mention Jesus' marriage, the birth of a child to Mary, or her connection to the sacred feminine. **See p. 87.**

LEONARDO DA VINCI & THE LAST SUPPER

Does Mary appear in Leonardo's painting of the Last Supper?	Art historians say no. The figure on Jesus' right is John the apostle, who is portrayed in a typical Renaissance fashion. **See pp. 89-91.**
Isn't the Holy Grail missing from the painting, confirming that the Grail is actually Mary?	Actually, no. The Bible does not mention the grail, but only a normal "cup" which Jesus passed to his disciples (and cups *are* present in the painting). The idea of a large bejeweled grail comes from later legend. **See p. 92.**
Is Peter threatening "Mary" in the Last Supper?	No. The painting portrays Peter leaning towards John in order to say the words recorded in John 13:24. The dagger in his hand is the sword he will use in John 18:10. **See p. 92.**
Does The Last Supper contain hidden messages related to the sacred feminine?	There is all kinds of symmetry in the painting, but none of it points clearly or conclusively to feminine symbolism. **See p. 91.**
Did Leonardo name the "Mona Lisa" after male and female deities?	No. Leonardo did not even name the painting. While the sitter is unknown, the name refers to Monna Lisa del Giocondo, the portrait's likely subject. **See pp. 93-94.**

THE PRIORY OF SION & THE KNIGHTS TEMPLAR

Was the Priory of Sion a secret society formed in Jerusalem in AD 1099 by King Godfrey de Bouillon?	No, the Crusader-era "Order of Our Lady of Zion" had nothing to do with the modern Priory of Sion, which was a political group created in France by Pierre Plantard and several friends in 1956. **See pp. 95-96.**
Was the purpose of the Priory to protect the secret of Jesus and Mary?	No, Plantard created the society to promote his pro-monarchical and anti-Semitic views. The society originally had nothing to do with Jesus or Mary Magdalene. **See p. 97.**

How did Plantard later use the Priory of Sion?	Plantard and several friends forged documents listing Grand Masters of the Priory and claiming that Plantard himself was the rightful heir to the throne of France. **See pp. 98-100.**
How did this legend get connected with Jesus and Mary Magdalene?	The authors of *Holy Blood, Holy Grail* brought together Plantard's list of Priory Grand Masters with a legend of lost treasure, claiming that the Priory's secret concerned Jesus' marriage to Mary Magdalene. **See pp. 100-102.**
Were the Knights Templar the military arm of the Priory?	No, the Knights were a monastic order formed in AD 1118 to protect Holy Land pilgrims during the Crusades. **See pp. 103-105.**
Did the Templars discover the Sangreal documents below the Jerusalem temple?	There is not a shred of reliable evidence that the Templars discovered anything under the temple ruins, whether Ark of the Covenant, Shroud of Turin, or Holy Grail. **See pp. 105-107.**
Did the Templars get rich by blackmailing the church about Jesus and Mary?	No, the Templars grew wealthy through gifts from wealthy patrons and as "bankers" for Europe's rich and powerful – not by keeping secrets about Jesus and Mary. **See pp. 103-104.**
Did Pope Clement V destroy the Templars to protect the secret of the Holy Grail?	No, it was king Philip IV of France who, out of desire for their wealth, conspired to destroy the Templars. **See pp. 104-105.**

ADDITIONAL RESOURCES

Books

Darrell L. Bock, *Breaking the Da Vinci Code. Answers to the Questions Everyone's Asking* (Nashville: Nelson, 2004). 188 pp.

An excellent work by a leading evangelical New Testament scholar. Not a point-by-point refutation of *The Da Vinci Code* but rather a response to its foundational historical and theological claims related to Jesus and the early church. Bock is research professor of New Testament at Dallas Theological Seminary and has a Ph.D. from the University of Aberdeen.

Ben Witherington III, *The Gospel Code: Novel Claims About Jesus, Mary Magdalene and Da Vinci* (Downers Grove, IL: InterVarsity, 2004). 208 pp.

Another excellent response by one of today's most prolific New Testament scholars. Witherington, like Bock, does not take on all the individual claims related to history and artwork of *The Da Vinci Code,* but responds to the historical, theological and philosophical foundations that lie behind it: questions of canon, the deity of Christ, Mary's place in the early church, the historical value of the Gospels, etc. Witherington is a professor of New Testament at Asbury Theological Seminary with a Ph.D. from the University of Durham.

Bart D. Ehrman, *Truth and Fiction in The Da Vinci Code. A historian reveals what we really know about Jesus, Mary Magdalene, and Constantine* (Oxford: University Press: 2004). 207 pp.

A well written response by an historian and biblical scholar who is not a conservative or an evangelical. This is a good text for those who are dubious of conservative Christian responses to *The Da Vinci Code* since it confirms that historians of all theological stripes find *The Da Vinci Code* seriously deficient in its portrayal of Jesus and Christian origins. Ehrman chairs the Department of Religious Studies at the University of North Carolina at Chapel Hill.

Carl E. Olson and Sandra Miesel, *The Da Vinci Hoax: Exposing the Errors in* The Da Vinci Code (Ignatius Press, 2004). 329 pp.

A very thorough and well written work from a Catholic perspective, which systematically debunks the fallacies of *The Da Vinci Code*. Miesel is a medieval historian and journalist and Olson is editor of *Envoy* magazine. This is the most comprehensive response to *all* the claims of *The Da Vinci Code* available today.

Josh McDowell. *The Da Vinci Code. A Quest for Answers* (Green Key Books, 2006).

An easy-to-read book presented as a dialogue between three friends who have just seen the movie. Well written and quite accurate, this is probably the best *Da Vinci Code* resource for young people.

Richard Abanes, *The Truth Behind the Da Vinci Code: A Challenging Response to the Bestselling Novel* (Harvest House Publishers, 2004). 96 pp.

A brief but well written and well organized response to many of the claims of *The Da Vinci Code.* Abanes is an author and journalist who focuses on religion and the cults.

Amy Welborn, *Decoding Da Vinci: The Facts Behind the Fiction of the Da Vinci Code* (Huntington, IL: Our Sunday Visitor, 2004). 124 pp.

A brief but helpful response from a Catholic author, written with a great deal of wit and in a lively engaging style. Not as well resourced or detailed as Olson and Miesel.

James L. Garlow & Peter Jones, *Cracking Da Vinci's Code: You've Read The Fiction Now Read the Facts* (Colorado Springs, CO: Victory, 2004). 252 pp.

An engaging response to *The Da Vinci Code* in the form of a narrative, where a young woman named Carrie wrestles with the questions raised by the book, especially those related to sexuality, feminism, the canon of Scripture, and the Gnostic Gospels. Garlow is the pastor of Skyline Wesleyan Church in Southern California, and has a Ph.D. in historical theology from Drew University. Jones is a professor at Westminster Seminary in California with a Ph.D. from Princeton Theological Seminary.

Hank Hanegraaff & Paul Maier, *The Da Vinci Code: Fact or Fiction* (Tyndale House, 2004). 81pp.

The first half of this short book, "The *Da Vinci* Deception," is written by Maier; the second part, "But What is Truth," is by Hanegraaff. A helpful work with a feisty tone. Maier is professor of ancient history at Western Michigan University with a Ph.D. from the University of Basel.

Hanegraaff is host of the *Bible Answer Man* radio program and president of the Christian Research Institute International (CRI), a Christian apologetic organization.

Michael Green, *The Books the Church Suppressed: Fiction and Truth in "The Da Vinci Code"* (Kregel, 2006). 192 pp.

A very good response to the claims of *The Da Vinci Code's* perspective concerning the canon of Scripture. Green is a prolific British evangelical author and scholar.

Erwin Lutzer, *The Da Vinci Deception: Credible Answers to the Questions Millions are Asking about Jesus, The Bible, and the Da Vinci Code* (Tyndale House, 2004). 122 pp.

A brief but insightful response written from a pastor's perspective.

Video

Lee Strobel and Garry Poole, *Discussing The Da Vinci Code* (DVD series; Zondervan, forthcoming).

A very helpful DVD curriculum designed for small group or individual study.

Television[1]

A number of well done television documentaries have been produced. While these present a balanced perspective, the alert observer will notice that when reputable scholars are consulted, they reject *The Da Vinci Code* as mostly fantasy. Some of these documentaries include:

Behind The Mysteries: Unlocking Da Vinci's Code - The Full Story. The National Geographic Channel (ABC News Productions). December 19, 2004. Produced by Jean Marie Condon and Yael Lavie; presented and written by Elizabeth Vargas.

The Real Da Vinci Code. Channel Four Television (Wildfire Television). February 3 2005. Produced by Simon Raikes; presented by Tony Robinson.

Secrets To The Code. Dateline: NBC (NBC Universal, Inc), April 13, 2005. Broadcast Producer, Elizabeth Cole; presented by Stone Phillips.

---

[1] These and other documentaries are discussed at the website http://priory-of-sion.com/dvc/documentaries.html